PAUL IN CONFLICT WITH THE VEIL

AN ALTERNATIVE INTERPRETATION OF 1CORINTHIANS 11:2-16

Thomas Schirrmacher

VTR
Publications

Bibliographic information published by Die Deutsche Bibliothek
Die Deutsche Bibliothek lists this publication in the Deutsche National-
bibliografie; detailed bibliographic data are available in the Internet at
http://dnb.ddb.de.

ISBN 978-3-933372-46-8

© 2007 by Thomas Schirrmacher
2nd edition

Translation: Cambron Teupe
Translated from the fifth German edition 2002
Cover Illustration: VTR Publications
Layout: VTR Publications
Printed in the UK by Lightning Source

Dedication

*"But we all, with open face beholding as in a glass the glory of
the Lord, are changed into the same image from glory to glory,
even as by the Spirit of the Lord."
(2Co 3:18)*

*"Nevertheless neither is the man without the woman, neither the
woman without the man, in the Lord. For as the woman is of the
man, even so is the man also by the woman; but all things of God."
(1Co 11:11-12)*

To Christine

Living and discussing with my counterpart,
daily strengthen my conviction
that the life-long marriage
of two human beings,
created by God to be essentially different,
is a divine covenant
and the climax of Creation.
Just as for the
Church, education, the economy and the State,
its significance for my personal
well being has no match.

.

TABLE OF CONTENTS

Foreword

While studying at the Free School of Theology in Basel, Dr. Schirrmacher and I were confronted with a seemingly insoluble problem. On the one hand, as Bible-believing Christians, we consider Scripture to be the infallible Word of God and reject the idea that the validity of its statements depends on culture. On the other hand, we treat 1Co 11:2-16 (the issue of headcoverings for women) as if this particular command of the Apostle Paul were no longer binding due to cultural changes. "With what justification," we asked ourselves, "do we declare some Scriptural statements to have been valid only in Bible times, and others to be binding for all cultures and times?" I find it essential to interpret the Bible according to a uniform hermeneutic system[1] rather than according to one's own preferences and tastes.

An article in the magazine *"Licht und Leben"*[2] brought us a little further. We discussed the issue, sometimes all trough the night, to discover whether the text of 1 Co 11 might include citations which Paul had quoted from a pre-vious Corinthian letter in order to contradict them. We used the "veil issue" as a test case.

I am now more convinced than ever that Paul indeed was addressing specific Corinthian arguments in order to refute them. This would have been no problem for the Corinthian church which knew its own position quite well. With careful exegesis, we can determine which statements are indeed such quotations. Our standard must be the Biblical text itself, not the fact that, "we cannot imagine" a certain statement. Whenever Paul apparently contradicts himself within few verses, we may assume that he is referring to the Corinthian arguments.

In the following book, Dr. Schirrmacher demonstrates how the application of this basic assumption to the veil issue in 1Co 11

---

[1] Hermeneutics is the „Doctrine of Understanding" of a text, that is, the basic, general rules, with which a text is to be interpreted. For the Bible, hermeneutics includes such questions as the insipiration of the Scripture, the relationship of the Old Testament to the New, the interpretation of parables, the usage of Old Testament quotations in the New Testament, etc.

[2] Paul Petry. „Das verschleierte Haupt", *Licht und Leben 67* (1956), pp. 52-54.

suggests a new[3] interpretation of the text. Even though some verses remain problematic (verse 10, for example), I find Schirrmacher's general direction convincing. The Bible-believing Christian who rejects any cultural invalidation of Scripture will find this approach helpful.

Should the following exegesis of 1Co 11 prove satisfactory, we should then examine other texts in 1Co to determine whether Paul uses the same stylistic device elsewhere, our standard being the Scriptural text itself The principle is that Biblical statements may be culturally limited in the form of their application, but not in their actual meaning.[4] It is essential, as the history of the interpretation of this text demonstrates, to avoid making one's own preconceptions the standard of interpretation, above all when dealing with other Pauline texts on the position of women in the Church and before God!

This book does not claim to answer all questions pertaining to the "veil issue", nor to all issues and problems which arise in 1Co or to Paul's opinion of women. Dr. Schirrmacher wishes to suggest an alternative interpretation of 1Co 11:2-16, in order to open new paths to understanding other texts in the book and other Pauline statements about women.

I hope this volume will have a wide circulation. May it help those who have been dissatisfied and prefer a hermeneutic which suits the text. May it also provide assistance to those open minded believers who want to learn, and are seeking a proper understanding of Biblical statements.

Dr. theol. Hans-Georg Wünch
Academic Dean and Lecturer of Hermeneutics,
Neues Leben Seminary, Wölmersen

---

[3] Not new in the sense that no one else has ever had this idea, but in the sense that it is no longer common, and is indeed somewhat unusual for modern readers.

[4] This applies also to Communion which was celebrated as a "Love Feast" which explains Paul's directions in 1Co 11:33ff. We do not need to change the form of Communion (which, however, would not be amiss), nor are Paul's statements meaningless for us today. The commandment to watch over and to be considerate of each other is still valid today. Only the form of the application has changed.

My Thanks

I would like to express my appreciation to **Dr. Hans-Georg Wünch**, **Dr. Jürgen Kuberski**, and to my father, **Prof. Bernd Schirrmacher**, for discussing similar, alternative interpretations of 1Co 11:2-16 with me and with supplying me with other material on the subject. My mother, **Ingeborg Schirrmacher**, and **Torsten Bissel** proofread the text of the first German edition. My wife, Christine, to whom I would like to dedicate this book, supported me with innumerable discussions on the general topic and on this book, itself. I cannot remember how often she has reread and supplemented the text over the years.

I also thank my translator **Cambron Teupe** who again has done a marvelous job and my coworker **Ron Kubsch** for organising the revision of the German and the making of the English edition.

Many librarians have offered more assistance than their job required. Particularly the following libraries have allowed me to use their literature and their space:

Library of the Philadelphia Theological Seminary, Philadelphia, PA (USA)

Library of the Westminster Theological Seminary, Philadelphia, PA (USA)

Library of the William Carey International University, Pasadena, CA (USA)

Bibliotheek van de Theologische Universiteit van de Gereformeerde Kerken
("Oudestraat"), Kampen (NL)

Bibliotheek van de Theologische Universiteit van de Gereformeerde Kerken
(Vrijgemakt), Kampen (NL)

British Museum Library, London (GB)

Bodleien Library, Oxford (GB)

New College Libray, Edinburgh (GB)

Free Church of Scotland College Library, Edinburgh (GB)

University Library, Edinburgh (GB)

Preface to the First German Edition

Only after long hesitation have I decided to have this book printed. This has four reasons:

1. I have close personal ties with many Christians all over the world who either believe that women ought to cover their heads, or understand 1Co 11:2-16 to indicate this practice. I do not want my interpretation to be understood as a personal attack or to instigate disagreements in individual congregations.

2. In suggesting this interpretation, I do not lay claim to absolute authority or knowledge, as many reservations in the text indicate. Still, I fear that some will misunderstand me in this way.

3. I do not want to be misunderstood as supporting a feminist view of Scripture. I have made sufficient statements on this subject in the past.

4. I do not wish to criticize the Word of God, merely to better understand what this Word says.

I therefore ask all readers to understand this book to be merely a contribution to a concrete exegetical and ethical issue, and not to jump to conclusions about my position on other issues, particularly those to which I have expressed an opinion elsewhere. I request a fair examination of my questions and reasoning, and would be glad to receive any correction of details, information on pertinent material or other suggestions, even though I may not be able to reply to all.

[DrThSchirrmacher@bucer.de]

Preface to the First English Edition

In the fifth German edition and the first English edition, I have made several changes, mostly in the third chapter. Above all I have discussed several articles and books printed after my first edition in 1993, responded to several reviews of my book and have expanded several arguments. The only major alteration is the shift of the discussion of the Jewish veiling custom which I have moved from Chapter 2 to Chapter 3.

Karl-Heinz Vanheiden accuses me of following the spirit of the times, for "This question has never been a problem for the last 1800 years."[5] He is right. The church generally ignored the issue for 1800 years, and never required women to cover themselves. If we apply to church history, we must examine not only theory but practice. Nor has the Church ever taught that men should have long hair, as we will see below.

Besides, the church's position has not been uniform during the last 1800 years, for the dispute on the interpretation began in the second century and has never ceased.[6] David E. Blattenberger points out that during church history, "Few pericopes in the New Testament have provided a basis for universal proclamation of obscurity on the one hand, and suprisingly similar lines of interpretation on the other."[7] Besides, Vanheidens view ignores other interpretations besides his and mine, for example the interpretation we will describe in detail that Paul is commanding women to wear long hair, not a headcovering.

---

[5] Karl-Heinz Vanheiden, "Thomas Schirrmacher. Paulus im Kampf gegen den Schleier ...," *Bibel und Gemeinde 99* (1999), p. 38.

[6] See Linda Mercadante, *From Hierarchy to Equality: A Comparison of Past and Present Interpretations of 1Cor 11: 2-16 in Relation to the Changing Status of Women in Society,* (Vancouver: G-H-M Books/Regent College, 1978) and Ralph N. Schutt, *A History of the Interpretation of 1Corinthians 11: 2-16,* (Dallas: MA Thesis Dallas Theological Seminary, 1978) (unpublished).

[7] David E. Blattenberger, *Rethinking 1Corinthians 11:2-16 through Archaeological and Moral-Rhetorical Analysis,* Studies in the Bible and Early Christianity vol. 36, (Lewiston: Edwin Mellen Press, 1997), p. 1.

How to Read this Book

The structure of this book allows the reader to decide for him-self how deeply he wishes to immerse himself in the material.

The first chapter presents the alternative interpretation of 1Co 11:2-16 in thirteen propositions without further discussion.

The second chapter discusses varying interpretations and the basic problem involved in the issue of women's headcovering.

The third chapter repeats the thirteen propositions and dis-cusses the alternative interpretation in more detail.

The fourth chapter deals with the general nature of the whole epistle 1Co and the possibility of finding other citations in it, par-ticularly in Chapter 5.

Finally, the fifth chapter discusses further New Testament statements about women.

I have tried to present my ideas in a style understandable to all readers. The notes and the paragraphs in small type discuss theological literature and indicate the representatives of other opinions. The reader himself must decide how intensively he wishes to study the material.

1. For the Reader in a Hurry: The Alternative View of 1Corinthians 11:2-16 in 13 Theses

1.1. The Thesis of this Book

This book proposes 1.) that the Corinthians' teaching that the woman must be veiled when praying (1Co 11:4-6); 2.) that men are forbidden to veil themselves (11:7); and 3.) that the woman is to live for her husband but not the husband for his wife (11:8-9), was derived from a misunderstanding of the Biblical teaching that the man is the head of the woman (1Co 11:3). In dealing with this question, according to the interpretation of this book, Paul first repeats the Corinthian position, then carries it to extremes (11:4-9), contradicts it (11:10-15) and finally explains that the veiling of the woman is not God's Law and thus not binding to all churches. In teaching the Biblical differentiation between man and woman (11:3), one may not draw conclusions which ignore the significance that the wife has for her husband, and which overlook the fact that "neither is the man independent of woman" (11:11).

1.2. An Alternative Translation of 1Corinthians 11:2-16

The following translation reflects this thesis. *The Corinthians' position is indented, Paul's opinion is not.*

Alternative Translation of 1Corinthians 11:2-16

(2) I praise you, however, that you remember me in all things and that you keep the traditions which I left you.
(3) I want you, however, to know that every man's head is Christ, but that every woman's head is her husband. Christ's head is God.

(4) Every man who prays or prophesies with anything hanging from his head disgraces his head.

(5) Every woman, however who prays or prophesies with a bare head disgraces her head, for she is then the same as one whose head is shaved.

(6) If a woman does not cover herself, then let her have her hair cut off.

Because, however, it is disgraceful for a woman to have her hair cut off or to be shorn, she should wear a veil.

(7) The man, of course, should not veil his head, for he is the image and glory of God; the woman is the glory of the man.

(8) The man does not come from woman, but the woman from man;

(9) for the man was not created for the woman's sake, but the woman for the man's sake.

(10) Therefore let the woman have authority over her head, because of the angels.[8]

(11) For in the Lord, neither is the woman without the man nor the man without the woman.

(12) For, just as the woman is from the man, so the man is also from the woman; but all are from God.

(13) Judge for yourselves!

It is fitting that a woman pray to God unveiled!

(14) Nature does not teach that it is indecent for a man to have (long) hair,

(15) but when a woman has (long) hair, it is an honor for her!

Her hair has been given to her instead of a veil.

(16) If, however, anyone finds it good to be quarrelsome, (let him consider that) we have no such custom, nor do the churches of God.

---

[8] Verse 10 can alternatively be indented as well, and should then be translated: "Therefore the woman should have an authority on her head, because of the angels."

An Alternative Translation of 1Corinthians 11:2-16
(structured)

Paul's interpretation

(2)   I praise you, however,
      that you remember me in all things and
      that you keep the   traditions
                       which I left you.
(3)   I want you, however, to know that
                every man's   head is   Christ,
                every woman's   head is   her husband.
                Christ's   head is   God.

The Corinthian's opinion

(4)   Every man
           who prays or prophesies
           with anything hanging from his head
                disgraces his head.
(5)   Every woman, however,
           who prays or prophesies
           with a bare head
                disgraces her head,
           for she is then the same
                as one whose head is shaved.
(6)   If a woman does not cover herself,
           then let her have her hair cut off.
      Because, however, it is disgraceful for a woman
           to have her hair cut off
           or to be shorn,
                she should wear a veil.
(7)   The man, of course,
           should not veil his head,
                for he is the image and glory of God;
      but the woman
           is the glory of the man.
(8)   For   the man   does not come from woman,
           but   the woman from man;
(9)   for   the man was
                not created for the woman's sake,
           but
           the woman for the man's sake.

Paul's opinion

(10)   Therefore let the woman
              have authority over her head,
                 because of the angels.

(11)   For,
          in the Lord,
              neither is the woman   without the man
              nor the man   without the woman.

(12)   For,   just as the woman   is from the man,
              so the man   I   is also from the woman;
                       but all are from God.

(13)   Judge for yourselves!
          It is fitting
                 that a woman pray to God unveiled!

(14)   Nature does not teach
              that it is indecent,
                 for a man to have (long) hair.

(15)   but when a woman has (long) hair,
                 it is an honor for her!
                 Her hair has been given to her
                 instead of a veil.

(16)   If, however, anyone finds it good
              to be quarrelsome, (let him consider that)
              we have no such custom,
              nor do the churches of God.

1.3. An Alternative Interpretation of 1Corinthians 11:2-16[9]

Surprisingly, most interpretations and applications of 1Co 11:2-16 for today generally consider only one of two alternatives; either that the woman must wear a veil when praying, or that this

---

[9] A preliminary, shorter presentation of these propositions can be found in "Paulus im Kampf gegen den Schleier." *Querschnitte 2* (1989): p. 2. An earlier sketch in "Bibelstellen, die Aussagen über die Frau beinhalten." *Gemeinde Konkret* (IWG: Erf-stadt/Bonn) Nr. 35 (Jan. 1985): pp. 9-10. The propositions presented here appeared in this form for the first time in "Paulus in Kampf gegen den Schleier: Eine alternative Auslegung von 1.Korinther 11,2-16." *AGORA: Krelinger Studenten Rundbrief Nr. 24* (Febr. 1992): pp. 26-31.

text is bound to its past cultural context and not applicable today. Few apparently realize that there are other interpretations according to which Paul is actually contradicting the command to use the veil at prayer.

I would therefore like to present one of these interpretations. **This thesis begins by considering the end of the text and then works forward to the beginning.**

Proposition 1

The text does not clarify what kind of "custom" Paul means. Only verse 15 names a concrete object, the *veil*, but the headscarf we know today is in any case a "modern" garment. If Paul is talking about an article of clothing at all, he does not mean a scarf, but a **veil** or a **cloak**. The expression, *"with anything hanging from his head"* (usually translated vaguely as "having something on his head") indicates this interpretation, as does the later Jewish and Middle Eastern custom of veiling. It is not clear whether the eyes and nose were covered, or – as most assume – they were free, as is the case with the "substitute veil", the hair.

Proposition 2

Few of those who teach that women should be veiled while praying have investigated the actual customs and clothing concerned. They correctly point out that Scripture, not one's own culture, must be the rule, and that 1Co 11:2-16 cannot be rejected just because it does not suit our culture. **We make exactly the same mistake, however, when we interpret Scripture from the standpoint of our own culture, by interpreting the text to describe our European article of clothing, the headscarf**, without investigating the actual historical custom. I doubt that any Christian defender of the headscarf would accept a complete veiling which would leave only eyes, nose and mouth free, for today.

Proposition 3

Of those who require headcovering for praying women, few have investigated the exact situation discussed in 1Co 11:2-16. Did the custom apply to Communion (as some believe), to prophetesses (as others believe), to church meetings, prayer meetings, or to a general everyday rule? It appears that these interpretations also tend to follow a cultural norm. This suspicion is strengthened by claims about the customs believed to be followed by the Romans, the Greeks or the Jews. There is, for example, no proof that Corinthian prostitutes had short hair, whereas ancient Roman, Greek and Jewish men all wore their hair long. The only reliable, admissible, cultural background for 1Co 11:2-16 is the Jewish custom (unknown in Old Testament times, however) that women were to be veiled in public.

Proposition 4

The only verse which mentions the veil (verse 15) states clearly, *"Her hair has been given to her instead of a veil."* **Whatever position Paul had been proposing before, his direction here clearly opposes veiling.** If he is recommending the veil in verses 2-14, then verse 15 means that the woman already has one. If he is opposing the veil, then verse 15 argues against it.

Proposition 5

The final verse supports this conclusion: *"[W]e have no such custom."* The *"custom"* which Paul rejects here is not quarreling (11:16) which was very common in Corinth, and which Paul in this very letter describes as sin, not as something out of the usual. The term *"custom"* here can only indicate the subject Paul has just been treating, the veil which we cannot describe more closely. **The Corinthians had a custom unknown to other Christian churches. If Paul rejects this custom, its details and interpretation have little significance for us.** We learn simply that a local church may not raise its own private customs to the status of Divine Law.

Proposition 6

Verses 13 and 14 are generally rendered as three rhetorical questions. **Since the original Greek text has no question marks, the reader can only distinguish questions by the use of interrogatives or from context**. Thus, these three sentences could equally well be rendered as statements: *"Judge for your-*

selves: It is decent for a woman to pray unveiled! Neither does Nature teach you that it is disgraceful for a man to have (long) hair, but an honor for a woman. " The second sentence even must be a statement, because the word *"oude"* never introduces a question. In this case, nature is not referred to as proof of Divine command – that would be unique in Scripture! On the contrary, it becomes quite clear that not nature can prescribe divine laws (but only the Word of God).

Proposition 7

Verses 11 and 12 refute verses 7 and 8, but agree with the description of Creation which verses 7 and 8 contradict, for the woman is just as much the *"image of God"* as the man. **If we assume that Paul is either repeating or exaggerating the Corinthians' position in verse 4-10, the problem is solved.** He uses this method frequently in 1 and 2Co (for example, 1Co 6:12-13; 7:1,5; 8:4-7,10,14-22, 2Co 12:11-15). Beginning with *"therefore"* in verse 10, Paul then introduces his reply and his refutation.

Proposition 8

Most of those who teach the alternative interpretations of 1Co 11:2-16 assume that Paul ends his repetition of the Corinthians' position in verse 9. **Verse 10 would then express his own opinion which gives the woman *"authority over her head"*. The formulation, "to have authority over" (*"exousia epi"*) is always used in this sense in the New Testament** (for example, authority over the demons) and is never used in the passive form ("to be subject to another's authority") and also never refers to one object lying on another. "To have authority over" means that the woman may decide for herself what she does with her head.

Proposition 9

Others who agree with the alternative interpretation add verse 10 to the Corinthian position, because of its seemingly inexplicable reference to the angels. According to this view, the *"authority over the head because of the angels"* in verse 10 need not be explained in reference to "lusting angels", but in reference to the

Jewish or Gnostic teachings which Paul continually fought in Corinth. For this reason, there is still no reasonable explanation for the reference to the angels. *The possibility that Paul mentions the angels because the Corinthians worshipped them, would correspond with the interpretation that verse 10 contains Paul's answer. Paul would therefore be pointing out, as in 6:3 that Christians, including women, would judge the angels, and that women, are therefore equally capable of deciding about their own heads.*

Proposition 10

Old Testament practice which describes both long-haired men, such as priests and Nazarites, and women who prayed unveiled, confirms the interpretation that Paul opposed both the veiling of women and the Corinthian rules about hair length. Veiling was not always a sign of honor, but could also have a negative significance. Thamar, for example, wore a veil to indicate that she was a prostitute (Ge 38:14-15).

Proposition 11

The theses 1-6 and 9-10 remain valid, even if propositions 7-8 are not.

Proposition 12

The text can thus be considered valid for our day and age, without causing confusion over an unknown custom. Paul always opposed the raising of traditions not commanded by the Word of God to the status of Divine Law, and thus taught in agreement with Jesus' words against the Pharisees in Mk 7:1-23. In no other place in the Old Testament or in the New does God command that a woman should be veiled, either at worship or otherwise. 1Co 11:2-16 is too controversial to be allowed such general consequences as the requirement that women must be veiled.

Proposition 13

The alternative interpretation of 1Co 11:2-16 presented here does not imply that Paul objects to the idea that men and women have different responsibilities – an idea which he himself teaches and defends. It does indicate, however, that the Corinthians had drawn the wrong conclusions from the correct statements in verse 3.

This would be typical of Paul's other arguments with the Corinthians, as the following two examples show. According to 1Co 5:9-13, several members of the church had wrongly assumed that church discipline required them to avoid private contact with the excommunicated member which Paul energetically refutes (1Co 5:10,12-13). Chapters 8 to 10 indicate that several Corinthians had misinterpreted the Biblical statement that there is only one God and that all other gods are nothing (8:4-7), to mean that they could participate in pagan sacrifices with a good conscience (8:7-11), a practice which Paul also refutes and opposes (10:14-22).

Summary (Repetition of 1.1)

The thesis of the following book is, therefore, that the Corinthians, drawing the wrong conclusions from the Biblical teaching that the man is head of the woman (11:3), had decreed that the woman must be veiled while praying (11:4-6), but that the man may not cover his head (11:7) and that a wife exists for her husband's sake, but not the husband for the wife's sake (11:8-9). After restating this position, Paul carries it ironically to its ridiculous, extreme conclusion (11:4-9), refutes it (11:10-15) and finally demonstrates that God had never commanded the veiling of the woman which is thus not binding on all believers. In teaching the Biblical distinction between man and woman, one may not draw conclusions about the value of the woman for the man, for the *"man without the woman"* (11:11) is no more than woman without the man.

2. The Most Difficult Text in the New Testament?

2.1 Between Misogyny and Egalitarianism

Do Uncovered Women Hinder Revival?

Are women's fashions one of "the greatest hindrances to re-vival" in the church?[10] Should Christians refuse to become women's hairdressers, since Scripture forbids women to wear short hair?

Christian Briem[11] assumes that a woman may pray only when her head is covered. Neither in the congregation, nor in the presence of her husband or children at home may she pray out loud. Besides, she must never cut her hair or wear it down, but must always put it up and cover it. Briem considers disobedience to this rule as sinful as adultery; wearing slacks as bad as murder. David Gooding[12] considers a woman without a head-covering "just as embarrassing to her husband as an adulteress."[13]

Most Christians would reject such a position in practice, if not in theory. But is Briem not justified, for he bases his teaching on 1Co 11:2-16 and 1Co 14:34-35? Shouldn't a woman who refuses to cover her head in church have a bad conscience, or at least the feeling that she is not doing justice to this part of Scripture, rejecting it as culturally antiquated? Do we not celebrate Communion which is also discussed in 1Co 11, even though our society shows less and less interest in such a tradition? Why are we unwilling to ignore our social environment by insisting that women cover their heads when they pray?

---

[10] Wim Malgo, "Welche Damengarderobe und Aufmachung beim Abendmahl?" *Mitternachtsruf 1* (1991): p. 22.

[11] Christian Briem, *Mann und Weib schuf er sie*, (Hückeswagen: Christliche Schriftenverbreitung): p. 66.

[12] David Gooding, "Symbole oder Zeichen von Autorität und Herrlichkeit", Das Thema 12, Beilage zu *Die Wegweisung 6/1987*, Christliche Verlagsgesellschaft Dillenburg, (Dillenburg, 1987): pp. 5-6.

[13] Ibid, p. 6.

The Difference Between Man and Woman

There is no question in my mind that God created man and woman with different characteristics and duties, and that marriage, with its mutual complementation of husband and wife, is the climax of Creation and the most important of its laws for all of mankind. To compel the abolition of these distinctions does not liberate woman, but forces her to deny her nature by either becoming a pseudo-man or a lesbian which, were it to become general practice, would wipe out mankind.

In the last few years an increasing number of secular scientists have begun to point out the essential differences between men and women. Professor of psychology, Wassilios E. Fthenakis, demands in his book *"Väter"*, for example, equal rights for men in the raising of children.[14] Studies on the human brain, such as Anne Moir's and David Jessel's *"Brainsex: der wahre Unterschied zwischen Mann und Frau"*[15], also support such conclusions.

In attempting to prevent the destruction of the family by applying Biblical principles on divorce, homosexuality, and "free" sex, however, the Christian must be sure that he is not substituting one error for the other, *but must apply the complete Biblical teaching and defend it from all attacks from the right as well as from the left. We may not swerve "to the right or to the left"*, as we shall see more clearly in the example of the Book of 1Co. *Should the reader, without having made the effort to examine the Biblical text closely, interpret my conclusions to be concessions to Feminism, he has completely misunderstood my intentions!* The Bible has played a significant role in the "liberation" of women, as an examination of other world religions and cultures shows. An accurate investigation of the Biblical view of Man and Woman can therefore be useful and should not be too quickly rejected as being inspired by the spirit of the times. (Is it not possible that a tra-

---

[14] Wassilios E. Fthenakis, *Väter* (Munich: Urban & Schwarzenberg, 1985).

[15] Anne Moir and David Jessel, *Brainsex: Der wahre Unterschied zwischen Mann und Frau* (Düsseldorf: Econ Verlag, 1990).

ditional view is just as dependent on the zeitgeist of its own culture?)

Women and Bible Translations

I believe that some translations and interpretations of Scripture have been influenced by an unchristian discrimination against women, for they unnecessarily rob them of the respect and tasks which Scripture gives them. A few examples for both will suffice:

One German translation renders **Heb 11:11** *"Durch Glauben empfing er auch mit Sara Kraft, Nachkommenschaft zu zeugen"*[16] (Through faith he received, together with **Sara**, the power to beget children.) "He", Abraham, is therefore the model of faith. A note adds,

"Perhaps the original wording of the Greek text is, 'Through faith, even Sara received power to conceive descendants, although she was barren.'"[17]

Although the translators themselves see Sara as the model of faith (along with Rahab in 11:31 and in verse 35 *"women"* in general), they have changed the text to infer that not Sara, but Abraham believed "with Sara". Is this not a case of Bible Criticism discriminating against women?

We find another example in the Old Testament story of Creation; God gives the man a *"helper"* (**Ge 2:18**; compare 2:20) "comparable" to him. Does the word "helper" mean a "housekeeper", one would like to ask? No, this term is always used in the Bible to refer to a person on whose assistance one is dependent – a person, therefore, superior in some way.[18]

---

[16] Die Heilige Schrift, Revised Elberfelder Bibel (Wuppertal: Brockhaus, 1986).

[17] Ibid., p. 281, Note 79.

[18] Alan Padgett, "Paul on Women in the Church: The Contradictions of Coiffure in 1Corinthians 11:2-16." *Journal for the Study of the New Testament 20,* (1984): pp. 69-86; Carl Schultz, 1598, *Theological Wordbook of the Old Testament*, Vol. 2, (Chicago: ed. R. Laird Harris, Moody Press, 1980), s. v. "azar"; U. Bergmann, *Theologisches Handwörterbuch zum Alten Testament*, vol. 2, ed. by Ernst Jenni, Claus Westermann (Munich: Chr. Kaiser Verlag, 1979), s. v. "zr helfen".

"An essential aspect of the meaning of verb and noun is that of combined effort or of the cooperation between subject and object, where the strength of one is insufficient ..."[19] The term is used approximately thirty times to refer to God ("You have been my help ... O God of my salvation!" **Ps 38:23**, 140:8).[20] Describing the woman as "helper" indicates that the man is in need of assistance. Dietrich Bonhoeffer writes: "God is man's only other support or help. Such a description of woman indicates something quite remarkable."[21]

Samuel R. Külling[22] and Elisabeth Hauser[23] both emphasize that the expressions, "helper" and "comparable" describe the woman in relationship to the man, but that this help is understood to be comprehensive and to include spiritual gifts. Elisabeth Hauser writes:

"Why 'may' a woman not also have intellectual abilities and education? Can she not complement her husband in this aspect as well? The Creation story designates no narrow pattern which forbids the woman the development of her personality in any area of life – rather the contrary would seem to be the case; in the word 'comparable to him' which (it seems to me) opens a wide horizon to her."[24]

Aida Dina Besancon Spencer points out that, in the first century, Jewish women were excluded from learning the Torah[25],

---

[19] Ibid.

[20] Ibid.

[21] Dietrich Bonhoeffer, *Schöpfung und Fall: Eine theologische Auslegung von Gen 1-3*, (Munich: Chr. Kaiser Verlag, 1958), quoted by Otto Dudzus, Ed., *Bonhoeffer Brevier* (Munich: Chr. Kaiser Verlag, 1963), p. 84.

[22] Samuel R. Külling, "Genesis 20. Teil 20: Gen 2,18-20", *Fundamentum* (FETA, 1985), vol. 4, pp. 7-18.

[23] Elisabeth Hauser, "Die Frau in Gottes Augen", op. cit., pp. 23-24.

[24] Ibid., p. 23.

[25] Aida Dina Besancon Spencer, "Eve at Ephesus (Should women be ordained as pastors according to the First Letter to Timothy 2:11-15)," *Journal of the Evangelical Theological Society 17*, (1974): pp. 215-222.

while Paul writes in 1Ti 2:11, a classical text on the role of women, *"Let a woman learn."*[26]

The word *"comparable"* (Ge 2:18) is derived from the word "to inform" which almost always means verbal information![27] Communication between husband and wife is a decisive *"help"* for life and a mark of their being comparable on the same level.

Ro 16:1 gives us a further example. Paul recommends Phoebe, the ***"deaconess"***, of the church in the Corinthian suburb of Cenchrea. Many translations do not express her actual office very clearly (The 1984 Luther translation, for example, refers to her as being *"in the service of the church"*), although the term "deacon" is otherwise used when referring to men. (Php 1:1, 1Ti 3:8,22).[28] (In all of the examples cited, I leave it up to the reader to decide whether the problem lies in the translation or in his or her interpretation.)

Phoebe is described here as *"our sister who is a deacon in the church in Cenchrea."* From the fact that the original text uses the masculine form of the word, one can deduce that Paul means a specific office which was also open to women. Besides, the addition, *"of the church in Cenchrea"*, would seem to indicate he is speaking of an office in a specific church and not of service in general.[29]

---

[26] Ibid.

[27] C. Westermann, *Theologisches Handwörterbuch zum Alten Testament*, vol. 2, ed. by C. Westermann and Ernst Jenni (Munich: Chr. Kaiser Verlag, 1979), s. v. "ngd hi. mitteilen".

[28] See Thomas Schirrmacher, *Das große Bibellexikon*, vol. 1, ed. by Helmut Burkhardt, (Wuppertal, 1987), s. v. "Diakon"; Thomas R. Schreiner, "The Valuable Ministries of Women in the Context of Male Leadership: A Survey of Old and New Testament Examples and Teaching", pp. 209-224 in John Piper and Wayne Grudem (Ed.), *Recovering Biblical Manhood and Womanhood* (Wheaton, Ill.: Crossway Books, 1991). Schreiner presents the arguments in favor of the office of deaconess in the New Testament (pages 213-214) and arguments against it (pages 219-220), although he sees the difference between deacons and elders in the exclusive teaching responsibility of the elders (1Ti 3:2,5).

[29] See Thomas Schirrmacher, *Der Römerbrief*, vol. 2, (Neuhausen: Hänssler, 1993[1]; Nürnberg: VTR / Hamburg: RVB, 2001[2]): pp. 300-301; Gerhard Lohfink, "Weibliche Diakone im Neuen Testament", *Diakonia 11*, (1980): pp. 385-400.

Besides, Phoebe is also called a *"prostatis"* ("Patroness": Ro 16:2) which emphasises her official role. The Greek word means "protectoress" or "patron"[30]. The corresponding form indicated a patron, a chairperson, a legal advisor.[31] The office of deaconness was well known in the Byzantine Church until the 11th century[32], and in Rome, Italy and the Western Church until the 5th and 6th centuries[33]. There is also documentation for the office in the West up until the 11th century[34]. The Monophysites had the office until the 13th century[35] and the Eastern church defended the office, following John Chrysostom, while the Western Church gave it up in order to avoid ordaining women, according to Ambrosiastes and Erasmus of Rotterdam[36]. These deaconesses definitely carried out spiritual duties. Elsie Anne McKee rightly says that there is heavy evidence that the deaconesses were employed by the church and were counted among the church officials.[37] They thus shared the status, privileges and restrictions of clerical persons such as the right to provisions[38], ordination[39] and celibacy,[40] and are mentioned in Canon 19 of the Council of Ni-

---

[30] Walter Bauer, Kurt und Barbara Aland, *Griechisch-deutsches Wörterbuch zu den Schriften des Neuen Testaments ...* (Berlin: W. de Gruyter, 1988[6]), Col. 1439.

[31] G. E. Benseler, Adolf Kaegi, *Benselers Griechisch-Deutsches Schulwörterbuch,* (Leipzig: B. G. Teubner, 1926[14]), p. 794.

[32] Adolf Kalsbach, *Die altkirchliche Einrichtung der Diakonissen bis zu ihrem Erlöschen*, Römische Quartalsschrift, Supplementheft vol. 22, (Freiburg: Freiburg, 1926), especially pp. 63-71, in which the author discusses the problems of wido whood, virginity and the office of deaconess in the Early Church.

[33] See L. Duchesne, *Christian Worship: Its Origin and Evolution: A Study of the Latin Liturgy up to the Time of Charlemagne*, (New York: Society for Promoting Christian Knowledge, 1931), pp. 342-343.

[34] Ibid., pp. 79-94 (in detail).

[35] Adolf Kalsbach, *Die altkirchliche Einrichtung der Diakonissen ...*, op. cit., pp. 59-60.

[36] See Elsie Anne McKee, *John Calvin on the Diaconate and Liturgical Almsgiving*, op. cit., pp. 161-163.

[37] Ibid., p. 65.

[38] Ibid., p 66.

[39] Ibid.

[40] Deaconesses, like the priests, were required to remain single which Protestants see as a possibility, but cannot consider a law. The necessity of remaining celibate proves that the office of deaconness was understood as a spiritual office.

caea for this reason.[41] Since the time of the early church, the specific responsibilities of the deacons and deaconesses have been drawn from Acts 6. The apostles distinguish between their responsibility, "to give ourselves continually to prayer and the ministry of the word" (Ac 6:4) and the duty to "serve tables" and to rule this business (Ac 6:2). Certain qualifications are required and an election is carried out. It is certainly authorized to use this as an example for the deaconate, for other cases in the Scriptures also discuss duties without clearly designating the "right" office. The duty is essential, not the title which may vary.

There has been much discussion whether the *"women"* mentioned in **1Ti 3:11** were the wives of the deacons or deaconesses; but the arguments in favor of the deaconesses seem more logical to me. It is significant that Paul provides no list of qualifications for the wives of the elders. Why should more be required of the deacons in reference to their wives, than of the elders?[42] The fact that the Scriptures give us a list of qualifications specifically meant for deaconesses, but not for female elders or overseers is compatible with the rest of New Testament teaching. Women may certainly carry responsibility in the church, but not as "fathers" of one or more congregations.

A further example can be found in **Ro 16:7**, in which Paul speaks of the apostles, Andronicus and Junia or Junias. Whether *"Junian"* is designated as a man or a woman depends more on the translator's opinion than on the word itself. C. E. B. Cranfield's Bible Commentary gives the most balanced representation.[43] Cranfield comes to the conclusion that *"Junian"*

---

[41] See Elsie Anne McKee, *John Calvin on the Diaconate and Liturgical Almsgiving*, op. cit., pp. 46-49.

[42] Ibid.

[43] C. E. B. Cranfield, *A Critical and Exegetical Commentary on the Epistle to the Romans*, vol. 2, The International Critical Commentary 11, Revision of 1979 Edition, (Edinburgh: T. & T. Clark, 1989): pp. 788-789. Compare Norbert Baumert, *Frau und Mann bei Paulus: Überwindung eines Mißverständnisses* (Würzburg: Echter Verlag, 1993): p. 187. Gerhard Lohfink, op. cit., Lohfink demonstrates that the name 'Junias' cannot be found being used for men elsewhere, and that the church fathers and theologians of the early church up into the Middle Ages held Junias to be a woman.

was probably Andronicus' wife, and, in any case, a female apostle in the sense that she was a representative of the churches, though not in the sense of the twelve apostles.[44]

The more general usage of the term "apostle" can be seen more clearly in **2Co 8:23**. Paul speaks of the "messengers" (or apostles) of the churches. Here the term refers to Paul's fellow workers on the mission field (Compare **Php 2:25**). They are not *"apostles of Jesus Christ"*, as the twelve disciples are called, but *"apostles of the church"* and correspond to our missionaries. Our word "missionary" comes from the Latin translation of the Greek word, *"apostle"* or *"messenger"*. **Ro 16:7** *is, as evidence, in my opinion, as valid as Paul's women helpers.*[45] This view is not merely a reaction to feminism[46], for the church father Chrysostom also believed that a woman apostle was meant.[47]

Another typical example is the expression used in **1Ti 5:14** for the woman's duties in *"managing the household"* which most translations reduce to "housekeeping". The Greek word is used as a verb only in the New Testament. As the designation of a person, **"the head of the house"** (Greek: *"oikodespotes"*), the word is composed of the word for "house" or "family" (Greek: *"oikos"*, origin of "economic") and "ruler" (Greek: *"despotes"*, origin of our "despot"), and is otherwise used to designate a man in a position of authority.

"In the New Testament, the word *'head of the house'* appears twelve times ... referring to the head of the house, the one who disposes over it. Frequently the Gospel of Matthew

---

[44] See also Schirrmacher, op. cit., pp. 300-301.

[45] John Piper and Wayne Grudem, ed., *Recovering Biblical Manhood and Womanhood* (Wheaton, Ill.: Crossway Books, 1991): pp. 79-81. The authors show that the church fathers disagreed on this point, and assume that the answer is insignificant, since the text is referring to apostles in the wider sense of the word which they translate as 'messenger'.

[46] Elizabeth Schüssler Fiorenza, *In Memory of Her* (New York, 1983): pp.226-230, presents a typically feministic interpretation of 1Co 11:2-16.

[47] William Danday and Arthur C. Headlam, *A Critical and Exegetical Commentary on the Epistles to the Romans*, vol. 11 of *The International Critical Commentary* (Edinburgh: T. & T. Clark, 1920): p. 423.

uses it in parables which compare God's activity with those of
the head of the house ... The word has its Semitic parallels, if
not its archetype in the frequent 'master of the house' which in
terms of the New Testament *'head of the house'* designates the
owner of the property."[48]

The same is true of the expression in **Tit 2:5**. Translated
"homemakers", the word can also mean *"managing the household"* or *"economical"* and is also used to refer to State business.[49] The final chapter of Pr (**Pr 31:10-31**) de-monstrates what
the Old Testament meant by this word.[50] The "excellent woman"
carries extensive authority, plans the economy of the household,
owns, buys and sells property; is known for her wisdom and
works six days a week, for God's command in the Ten Commandments, *"Six days shalt thou labor..."* is just as valid for her
as for any other human being (Ex 20:9 describes not only salaried
labor, but work in general).

Besides, the **"house"** of **1Ti 5:14** and **Tit 2:4-5** can hardly be
understood to be the building, but according to the usage of both
Old and New Testaments, describes the **extended family. The
particular responsibility of the wife is defined in terms of the
family, not of the domicile.** This agrees then with the order
given in both verses: **The wife's first duty is to her husband,
then to her children, and finally to the "house", the extended
family**. In 1Ti 5:14 *bearing children* and *managing the household* follow *marriage* and the relationship to the husband; in Tit
2:4-5, Paul commands the woman to love her *husband* first, next
her *children*, and finally *to be chaste and a good housewife (or*

---

[48] Karl-Heinrich Rengsdorf in *Theologisches Handwörterbuch zum Neuen Testament*,
vol. 2, ed. by Gerhard Kittel, (Stuttgart: W. Kohlhammer, 1990), s. v. "oikidespotes".
See also: Walter Bauer, Kurt and Barbara Aland, *Wörterbuch zum Neuen Testament*,
(Berlin: Walter de Gruyter, 1988). Katharine Bushnell, *101 Questions Answered: A
Woman's Catechism-God's Word to Women*, (Southport: Lowes Ltd., G. B., 1930): pp.
68-69.

[49] G. E. Benseler, Adolf Kaegi. *Benselers Griechisch-Deutsches Schulwörterbuch*,
(Leipzig: B. G. Teubner, 1926): p. 636.

[50] See David Alan Hubbard, "The Stereotyped Female", *Theology, News and Notes*
(Pasadena: Fuller Theological Seminary Alumni, June 1975): pp. 9-13.

manager) and kind. The woman is thus not to live in and for her home, but with and for her family.

This does not exclude that the living space does not play a central role in her duties toward her family, as Dietrich Bonhoeffer so fittingly writes:

"The place God has designated for the wife is her husband's home. Many have forgotten its meaning nowadays, but it has become very clear to others of us in this day and age. In the center of the world, it is its own kingdom, a fortress in the storm, a refuge, even a sanctuary ... It is God's foundation in the world, the place where – whatever may happen in the world – peace, quiet, joy, love, purity, discipline, respect, obedience, tradition and with all that, happiness should dwell."[51]

For this reason, Pr 14,1 tells us, *"The wise woman builds her house."* Likewise, the man in Ps 128, 2-4, blessed *"by the labor of his hands"*, is also blessed in his wife who is *"like a fruitful vine in the very heart of his house"* and whose children are like *"olive plants all around his table"*.

Many translations of the New Testament address long paragraphs, even whole chapters, exclusively to the **"brethren"** although women are specifically addressed as well[52], as in 1Co 11:2-16 or Php 4:1-3. **"Brothers and sisters"** or "Siblings" would, however, be a more accurate translation. Most languages designate the children of the same parents by the plural of either the feminine or the masculine children. German uses the plural of the feminine, English of the masculine children. In Greek, the masculine form (*"adelphoi"*) is used to designate the male and female children of one family and not the feminine form "sisters" (*"adelphai"*). *New Testament statements addressing "brethren" also include women.*

---

[51] Dietrich Bonhoeffer, *Widerstand und Ergebung: Briefe und Aufzeichnungen aus der Haft* (Munich: Chr. Kaiser, 1958): pp. 44-45. See also pp. 44-46.

[52] See Gordeon D. Fee, *The First Epistle to the Corinthians, The New International Commentary on the New Testament* (Grand Rapids, Mi.: Wm. B. Eerdmans, 1987): p. 52, note 22.

Even the Greek word *"aner"* (Man) does not always signify the male gender, unless required by the context. It can mean "the human race"[53] and generally refers to human beings, inhabitants or people, and in the plural often to groups of people including men and women.[54] The New Testament also uses the term in this sense (Mt 14:35; Lk 3:11; 11:31; Jn 6:10; Ac 4:4; 2:5,14). According to Oepke, the meaning "human being" is more frequent than generally realised.[55] Texts which describe angels appearing in the form of "men" (Heb 13:2; Jn 20:12; Ac 1:10; 10:30 and frequently in the Greek translation of the Old Testament), do not, therefore, prove that they were male. Ac 17:14 demonstrates clearly that *"aner"* could include men and women: "Some of the Jews were persuaded and joined Paul and Silas, as did a large number of God-fearing Greeks and not a few prominent women."

In **Tit 2:3**, Paul admonishes the *"older women" "likewise that they be reverent in behavior, not slanderers, not given to much wine, teachers of good things"*. The word rendered as ***"reverent"*** (Greek: *"hieroprepes"*) in the New King James Version, consists of the word "prepes" ("proper") and the word *'hieros'* ('priest'). Why should the translation not make it clear that the older women have a priestly duty? If the general priesthood of believers includes all Christians, then it includes women as well. Joachim Jeremias renders the text, *"Admonish the older women, likewise,*

---

[53] J. B. Bauer. "aner ...". Col. 236-238 in: Horst Balz, Gerhard Schneider (Ed.), *Exegetisches Wörterbuch zum Neuen Testament*, 2 Vols, Vol 1, (Stuttgart: W. Kohlhammer, 1992²), Col. 236; see also Albrecht Oepke, "aner", pp. 362-364 in: Gerhard Kittel (Ed.), *Theological Dictionary of the New Testament,* 10 Vols, (Grand Rapids: Wm. B. Eerdmanns Publishing Co., 1983 [repr. 1964]), Vol I, p. 360: "The word is also used for the human species."

[54] See the examples in Heinz Külling, *Geoffenbartes Geheimnis: Eine Auslegung von Apostelgeschichte 17,16-34*, Abhandlungen zur Theologie des Alten und Neuen Testaments vol. 79, (Zürich: Theologischer Verlag, 1993), pp. 165-166 and Albrecht Oepke, "aner", op. cit., p. 361.

[55] Albrecht Oepke, "aner", op. cit., p. 362.

that they be priestly in their behavior (translation: C.T.). "[56] Donald Guthrie interprets *"hieroprepeis"*

> "meaning 'consecrated as priestesses', an idea well captured by Lock who gives the meaning, 'they carry into daily life the demeanour of priestesses in a temple'"[57].

Gottfried Holtz suggests that the reminder of the older women's priestly responsibility and the warning against drunkenness could be a deliberate reference to the drunken priestesses of the Bacchus cult.[58] Martin Dibelius writes,

> "[W]hen one considers the emotionalism characteristic of the parallel text in ITim. 2:10. ... 'Christian women are holy women'. ... one tends to see a challenge to the older women to have a certain 'priestly' dignity ..."[59]

When we take the time to examine such examples, we begin to understand the value of a careful examination of the Scriptures dealing with the duties and the role of women, as this book will attempt to do.

---

[56] Joachim Jeremias and August Strobel, *Die Briefe an Timotheus und Titus, Der Brief an die Hebräer*, vol. 9 of *Neues Testament Deutsch* (Göttingen: Vandenhoeck and Ruprecht, 1982): p. 1: "die älteren Frauen ermahne gleichfalls, daß sie priesterlich seien in ihrer Haltung." See also G. Wohlenberg, *Die Pastoralbriefe*, vol. 13 of *Kommentar zum Neuen Testament* (Leipzig: A. Deichert, 1906): pp. 229-230; E. P. Scott, *The Pastoral Epistles*, vol. 13 of *The Moffatt New Testament Commentary* (London: Hodder and Stoughton, 1956): pp. 163-164; Richard and Catherine Clarke Kroeger, *I Suffer not a Woman: Rethinking 1Timothy 2:11-15 in the Light of Ancient Evidence* (Grand Rapids, MI: Baker Book House, 1992): p. 91.

[57] Donald Guthrie, *The Pastoral Epistles*, vol. 14 of *Tyndale New Testament Commentary* (London, 1957): p. 192, citing Walter Lock, *The Pastoral Epistles, International Critical Commentary*, T. & T. Clark (Edinburgh, 1936): p. 140. Lock adds that women should live in a "temple-like" manner and supports his view with Jewish and Greek parallels.

[58] Gottfried Holtz, *Die Pastoralbriefe*, vol. 13 of *Theologischer Handkommentar zum Neuen Testament* (Berlin: Evangelische Verlagsanstalt, 1980): p. 219.

[59] Martin Dibelius and Hans Conzelmann, *Die Pastoralbriefe, Handbuch zum Neuen Testament* (Tübingen: J. C. B. Mohr, 1955): p. 105.

2.2 Interpretation Without End?

Problem After Problem

1Co 11:2-16 is possibly the most difficult text in the New Testament, one which has not only inspired a flood of interpretations,[60] but which contains in almost every verse some controversial problem.[61] It is "one of the most obscure passages in the Pauline letters "[62]. These verses "still await a really convincing explanation"[63] and:

"It could not be said that the passage has surrendered his mystery."[64]

And Thomas R. Schreiner writes:

"First Corinthians 11:2-16 has some features that make it one of the most difficult and controversial passages in the Bible."[65]

The evangelical exegete Gordon D. Fee writes: "This passage is full of notorious exegetical difficulties."[66] He groups them as follows: 1. the logic of the whole, 2. the question which habit lies behind the text, and 3. "our uncertainty about the meaning of some absolutely crucial terms,"[67] which he lists as "head" (vv. 3-4); "having down the head" (v. 4); "uncovered" (vv. 5, 13);

---

[60] On the history of the interpretation of the passage, see Linda Mercadante, *From Hierarchy to Equality: A Comparison of Past and Present Interpretations of 1Cor 11:2-16 in Relation to the Changing Status of Women in Society* (Regent College: G-H-M Books, Vancouver, 1978). Mercadante investigates the most important interpretations since Calvin (1546) and modern feminist interpretations. Ralph N Schutt, *A History of the Interpretation of 1Corinthians 11:2-16,* MA Thesis, (Dallas: Dallas Theological Seminary, 1978). Lacks a complete bibliography. Only those texts which the author cites are listed, not all works consulted.

[61] See the summary of the various interpretations in Antoinette Clark Wire, *The Corinthian Woman Prophets* (Minneapolis: Fortress Press, 1990): p. 278.

[62] Wayne Meeks, *The Writings of St. Paul,* (New York: Norton, 1972), p. 38.

[63] C. D. Moule, *Worship in the New Testament* (London: Lutterworth, 1961): p. 65.

[64] G. B. Caird, "Paul and Women's Liberty", *Bulletin of the John Rylands Library 34* (1972): pp. 268-281.

[65] Thomas R. Schreiner, "Head Coverings, Prophecies and the Trinity: 1Corinthians 11:2-16", *Recovering Biblical Manhood and Womanhood,* ed. by John Piper and Wayne Grudem, (Wheaton, Il, 1991): p. 124.

[66] Gordon D. Fee, *The First Epistle to the Corinthians,* op. cit., p. 492, Note 4.

[67] Ibid.

"glory" (v. 7); "authority over the head" (v. 10); "because of the angels" (v. 10); "in the place of a shawl" (v. 15); "such a custom" (v. 16). For historical-critical theologians, this text is thus one of the weakest of Paul's achievements. Robin Scroggs, for example, writes: "In its present form this is hardly one of Paul's happier compositions."[68]

And Christian Wolff adds: "The details of Paul's arguments against the Corinthians' pneumatic enthusiasm are not very convincing."[69]

Those who reject such an attitude toward the Scriptures, however, cannot simply ignore the problem. *The interpretation seems obvious only when using translations which have already decided on the meaning of the text; the original Greek text is not so unambiguous.*

Nor do I hold my interpretation to be *the last word*; I will myself point out its weaknesses, as well as *variations of the model* and other possibilities.

Evangelical and fundamentalist authors treat 1Co 11:2-16 in different and often unsatisfactory ways. Although most believe Paul to be insisting on the wearing of a head covering, they reject his instructions as culturally obsolete.[70] This is true even of those decided defenders of the traditional understanding of the New

[68] Robin Scroggs, "Paul and Eschatological Woman", *Journal of the American Association for Religions* (JAAR) 46 (1972): pp. 283-303, here p. 297.

[69] Christian Wolff. "Der erste Brief des Paulus an die Korinther. Zweiter Teil: Auslegung der Kapitel 8-16," *Theologischer Handkommentar zum Neuen Testament* VII, (Berlin: 2. Evangelischer Verlagsanstalt, 1982): p. 68.

[70] For example, the three best-known Evangelical commentaries in the German language. 1) Werner de Boor (ed.), "Der erste Brief des Paulus an die Korinther", *Wuppertaler Studienbibel*, op. cit., pp. 178-185. "We must consider that Paul is not writing an eternally valid theological treatment of the subject ..." And this with no explanation. 2) Heiko Krimmer, "Erster Korinther-Brief," vol. 11 of *Bibel-Kommentar* (Neuhausen: Hänssler Verlag, 1985): pp. 242-250. 3) Normann Hillyer, "Der erste und zweite Brief an die Korinther", Ibid., p. 327. See also Friedrich Godet, *Kommentar zu dem ersten Briefe an die Korinther*, Part 2 (Hannover: Verlag Carl Meyer, 1888) and Friedrich Lang, *Die Briefe an die Korinther. Das Neue Testament Deutsch* 7 (Göttingen: Vandenhoeck & Ruprecht, 1986).

Testament texts about women, writers who otherwise rightly reject a cultural explanation.[71] Representatives of the view that
women should wear a head scarf when praying have criticized
this inconsistency.[72]

According to Charles Hodge, Paul intends women to dress according to the taste of their society.[73] Such a statement would
have been understandable in the middle of the last century, but
Hodge would hardly choose the taste of the modern fashion mak-
ers for the criterion for Christian decorum, as Normann Hillyer
has recently done,[74] without explaining what could be considered
decent nowadays and which of the many tastes of our societies is
to be the norm.

As I have said, particularly Evangelical and Fundamentalist
authors decidedly reject this approach. An article in the Journal of
the Evangelical Theological Society by Grant R. Osbourne demonstrates the establishment of one's own hermeneutic principles
for 1Co 11:2-16 which Evangelicals themselves otherwise criticize. Before discussing New Testament references to women,
Osborne gives seven principles for interpretation, including the
one he uses to solve the problem in 1Co 1:2-16:

"The tools of redaction criticism will help distinguish what
comes from early Church tradition from what was a temporary
application to a specific problem. ... Teaching that transcends
the cultural biases of the author and his readers will be normative. ... Those commands that have proven detrimental to the
cause of Christ in later cultures must be reinterpreted."[75]

---

[71] Particularly evident in John Piper and Wayne Grudem (ed.), *Recovering Biblical
Manhood and Womanhood* (Wheaton, Ill.: Crossway Books, 1991): pp. 74-75, and
Thomas R. Schreiner. "Head Coverings, Prophecies and the Trinity," op. cit., p. 138.

[72] Bruce K. Waltke, "1Corinthians 11:2-16: An Interpretation", *Bibiotheca Sacra* no.
537: 135 (1978): pp. 46-57.

[73] Charles Hodge, *A Commentary 1 & 2Corinthians* (Edinburgh: The Banner of Truth
Trust, 1988): p. 205.

[74] Norman Hillyer, op. cit., p. 327. The application of this principle will vary from
place to place and from time to time, and will orient itself on what is currently considered decent.

[75] Grant R. Osborne, "Hermeneutics and Women in the Church", *Journal of the Evangelical Theological Society 20* (1977): pp. 337-352, here p. 339.

It is easier for other Christian groups to distinguish between the (supposedly) apostolic ruling and modern practice. For the Catholic, J. P. Meier, for example, 1Co 11:2-16 is proof that the Church may and does deviate from it.[76]

A Bouquet of Interpretations

A small sample of various interpretations of the whole text should serve to demonstrate the number of questions still to be solved, as well as the implausibility of any attempt to interpret the text merely by simply reading the English translation with the attitude "That's what it says".

I have already mentioned Christian Briem. Albert Löscher believes that Paul is teaching that a woman may not cut her hair, but needs no scarf, because her hair has been given to her as a covering (Verse 15).[77]

The veil is not a symbol of submission, according to A. Pérez Gordo and Ernst Lerle, but the woman's honor which she must therefore wear.[78]

P. Cürlis gives the text the title "Man, Woman and Family Devotions".[79] He sees in this Scripture the rule that the difference between man and woman should be adapted to local custom[80], guided by natural feelings.

R. E. Oster believes that Paul is opposing the introduction of Roman custom of covering men's heads at sacrifices or other religious activities.[81]

William MacDonald believes the text to refer to the church service, but not to home group meetings. He offers no evidence

---

[76] J. P. Meier, "On the Veiling of Hermeneutics (1Corinthians 11:2-16)," *The Catholic Biblical Quarterly 40* (1978): pp. 212-226, here pp. 339-340.

[77] Albert Lüscher, *Verschnittene Haare in biblischer Sicht* (Langenthal: Pflugverlag).

[78] A. Pérez Gordo, "¿Es el velo en 1Co 11,2-16 símbolo de libertad o de submisión?" Burgense 29, (1988): pp.337-366; Ernst Lerle, op. cit.

[79] P. Cürlis, "Der erste erhaltene Brief Pauli an die Korinther," in *70 Stunden ausgelegt für Gemeinde und Gemeinschaft* (Neumünster: G. Ihloff, 1926): pp. 431-444.

[80] Ibid., pp. 443-444.

[81] R. E. Oster, "When Men Wore Veils to Worship: The Historical Context of 1Corinthians 11:4," *New Testament Studies* 34, (1988): pp. 481-505.

for his interpretation, but only says, "The author tends to believe ..."[82] which is typical of this view.

Wilhelm Busch assumes that the text refers only to married women and warns against offences against decency.[83]

According to A. Isaksson, the text refers only to married prophetesses who were to wear their glory only when prophesying.[84] Because of the close relationship between the prophetic office and the Nazirite vow, prophetesses had to have long hair, just as the Nazirites did.[85]

Ray Sutton assumes that only prophetesses need a head covering when praying or prophesying, and that, since prophecy ceased in 70 AD, the text is irrelevant for the modern church.[86]

James B. Jordan shares this view, but adds that no one can obey 1Co 11:2-16 anyway, since no one knows what Paul means, and whether he was requiring a veil, a scarf or long hair.[87]

William J. Martin limits Paul's injunction to the Lord's Supper[88] For N. R. Lightfoot the text deals only with congregational meetings[89],

---

[82] William MacDonald, *1.Korintherbrief* (Dillenburg: Emmaus Fernbibelschule, 1971): pp. 16.

[83] Wilhelm Busch, "Zopf und Bibel," *Licht und Leben 67* (1956) pp. 20-20.

[84] Abel Isaksson, *Marriage and Ministry in the New Temple: A Study with Special Reference to Mt. 19.3-12 and 1Cor. 11.3-16* (Lund: Hakan Ohlsson, 1965): pp. 155-188. See also the review by Heinrich Baltensweiler, "Abel Isaksson, Marriage and Ministry in the New Temple ...," *Theologische Zeitschrift 23* (1967): pp. 356-358.

[85] Abel Isaksson. *Marriage and Ministry in the New Testament.* op. cit., pp. 172 and 189-198.

[86] Ray Sutton, "The Covenantal Structure of ICorinthians: Part II," *Covenant Renewal* (Tyler/TX) 2 (1988): No. 11. pp. 1-4, here pp. 3-4.

[87] James B. Jordan, "The Woman's Head Covering in 1Corinthians 11:2-16," *Biblical Horizons No. 54* (Oct 1993), pp. 1-4.

[88] William J. Martin, "1Corinthians 11:2-16: An Interpretation," in W. Ward Gasque, Ralph P. Martin (ed.), *Apostolic History and the Gospel* (FS F. F. Bruce), (Grand Rapids: Wm B. Eerdmans): pp. 232-233; G. L. Almie, "Women's Church and Communion Participation: Apostolic Practice or Innovative Twist?" *Christian Brethren Review 33* (Exeter: Paternoster Press, 1982): pp. 41-35. By referring to 1Co 14:34-35 as a teaching function, Almie resolves the apparent contradiction between these two texts.

[89] N. R. Lightfoot, "The Role of Women in Religious Services," *Restoration Quarterly 19* (1976): pp. 129-136.

for F. W. Grosheide not only with congregational meetings, but in general.[90]

N. Weeks considers the headcovering necessary only for women in positions of responsibility when exercising their office.[91]

The Paktistani Christian Christine Amjad-Ali finds it difficult to apply 1Co 11:2-16 to the discussion on the proper Christian reaction to the Islamic veil.[92]

Is it Just a Question of Long Hair?

In order to be fair, I should mention that not all writers, not even all those Evangelical writers who believe that women require no headcovering when praying, assume that the text commands a scarf, but considers the admonition to be irrelevant in our society. Besides those who interpret the text as I do, there are other Evangelicals who assume that Paul himself required no headcovering. James B. Hurley[93], the most important representative of this group, attempts to demonstrate that the text has nothing to do with the veil, but only with long hair. The woman's hairstyle must distinguish her from the man. He has won the approval of many exegetes.[94]

---

[90] F. W. Grosheide, *De Eerste Breif aan die Ker to Korinthe, Commentar op het Newuwe Testament* (Kampen: J. H. Kok, 1957): pp. 290-291.

[91] N. Weeks, "Of Silence and Head Covering", *Westminster Theological Journal 35* (1972): pp. 21-27.

[92] Christine Amjad-Ali, *Dare to Dream: Studies on Women and Culture with reference to ICorinthians 11:2-16*, CSC Monograph vol. 25, (Rawalpindi (Pakistan): Christian Study Center/Women in Reflection and Action, 1990).

[93] James B. Hurley, "Did Paul Require Veils or Silence of Women? A Consideration of 1Co 11:2-16 and 1Co 14:33b-36," *Westminster Theological Journal 35* (1973): pp. 190-220; James B. Hurley, *Man and Woman in Biblical Perspective* (Grand Rapids: Zondervan, 1981): pp. 162-184. Hurley considers the hairstyle to be a cultural matter and concludes that men and women ought to dress so as to be distinguishable.

[94] Norbert Baumert, *Antifeminismus bei Paulus?: Einzelstudien* (Würzburg, Germany: Echter Verlag, 1992): p. 56; Alan Padget, "Paul on Women in the Church: The Contradictions of Coiffure in 1Corinthians 11.2-16," *Journal for the Study of the New Testament 21* (1984): pp. 69-86; Jerome Murphy-O'Connor, "1Corinthians 11:2-16 Once again," *The Catholic Biblical Quarterly 50* (1988): pp. 265-274; Jerome Murphy-O'Connor, "Sex and Logic in 1Corinthians 11:2-16," *The Catholic Biblical Quarterly 50* (1988): pp. 482-500; Daniel L. Segraves, *Hair Length in the Bible. A Study of I Corinthians 11:2-16*, (Hazelwood: World Aflame Press, 1989) (first edition 1973 under

Until the 1950's, all agreed that the text intended women to wear a veil, but the extent of this article of clothing was unclear: Was the garment to cover only the hair or the face as well? Or should the garment cover the whole body? In the 50's, a few theologians began to suggest that Paul was demanding long hair rather than a veil.[95] In 1965, Abel Isaksson submitted the first exegetical support for this view.[96] The expression *"kata kephales echon"* ("to have something hanging from the head") which was sometimes used in Greek literature to describe a woman's long, flowing hair (not pinned up), played a major role in his argument. The text does not mention a specific garment, the arguments goes[97], except in verse 15 which compares the woman's hair to a veil (which is definitely an article of clothing – whatever Paul meant, he does speak of a garment).

Using Rabbinical sources, the Jewish historian Samuel Krauss has attempted to demonstrate that the expression "to cover" actu-

---

the title *Women's Hair – The Long and Short of It*); David E. Blattenberger, *Rethinking 1Corinthians 11:2-16 through Archaeological and Moral-Rhetorical Analysis*, Studies in the Bible and Early Christianity, vol. 36, (Lewiston: Edwin Mellen Press, 1997), esp. pp. 27-38, Gijs Bouwman, "Het hoofd van de man is de vrouw' Een retorische analyse van 1Kor 11,2-16," *Tijdschrft voor Theologie 21* (1981): pp. 28-36; Gérard Pella. "Viole et Soumission?: Essai d'interpretation de deux textes pauliniens concernant le statut de l'homme et de la femme," *Hokma 30* (Lausanne, 1985): pp. 3-20; Dorothy Pape, *Wir Frauen und Gott* (Marburg, Germany: Verlag der Francke-Buchhandlung, 1981): pp. 76-89; Abel Isaksson, *Marriage and Ministry in the New Testament*, op. cit., pp. 165-186; Alan Padgett, "Paul on Women in the Church", op. cit., p. 70; William J. Martin, *"1Corinthians 11:2-16,"* op. cit., p. 233; Hans-Josef Klauck, *Erster Korintherbrief. Die Neue Echter Bibel 7* (Würzburg, Germany: Echter Verlag, 1984): pp. 78-80. Further advocates are listed in Jason David BeDuhn, "Because of the Angels: Unveiling Paul's Anthropology in 1 Corinthians 11," *Journal of Biblical Literature 118* (1999) pp. 295-320, pp. 296-297, Note 7.

[95] See Ralph N. Schutt, *A History of the Interpretation of 1Corinthians 11: 2-16,* (Dallas: MA Thesis Dallas Theological Seminary, 1978) (unpublished), pp. 73-75; Linda Mercadante, *From Hierarchy to Equality: A Comparison of Past and Present Interpretations of 1 Cor 11: 2-16 in Relation to the Changing Status of Women in Society,* (Vancouver: G-H-M Books/Regent College, 1978), p. 82 and David E. Blattenberger, *Rethinking 1Corinthians 11:2-16 through Archaeological and Moral-Rhetorical Analysis,* op. cit., pp. 2-3.

[96] Abel Isaksson, *Marriage and Ministry in the New Temple: A Study with Special Reference to Mt. 19.3-12 and 1. Cor 11.3-16,* (Lund: Hakan Ohlsson, 1965).

[97] See esp. Daniel L. Segraves, *Hair Length in the Bible,* op. cit., pp. 22-23.

ally refers to pinning the hair up.[98] Paul would therefore be commanding women to put up her hair, so that it did not hang down loose.

These explanations share the result of our interpretation, namely that Paul doesn't require headcovering and a veil. Nevertheless these interpretations depart from ours, as they insist that women wear their hair long and either falling down or pinned up, an idea then usually rejected on the basis of its cultural irrelevance. These interpretations thus only function partially without the argument that Paul's directions are culturally restricted.

---

[98] Samuel Krauss, "The Jewish Rite of Covering the Head," op. cit., pp. 159-160.

3. The Alternative View in Detail

3.1 The Alternative Interpretation is Nothing New

There have been various versions of the alternative view; that Paul first repeats his opponent's view, draws it to ridiculous conclusions, and then refutes it, thus not commanding but contradicting the requirement for the veil.[99]

---

[99] **A chronological listing of representatives of the citation interpretation of 1Co 11:2-16, as far as known to me:**

John Lightfoot. *The whole Writings of the Rev. John Lightfoot ... Volume XII containing Horae Hebraicae et Talmuidicae or Hebrew and Talmudical Exercitations upon the Gospels of St. Luke and St. John, upon some few Chapters of the Epistle to the Romans the The First Epistle to the Corinthians.* (Printed London: J. F. Dove, 1823, written 1675);

John Lightfoot. *A Commentary on the New Testament from the Talmud and Hebraica,* vol. 4 (Peabody, Mass.: Hedrickson Publ, 1990): pp. 229-241;

Katharine Bushnell, *God's Word to Women* (Oakland, Cal., written maybe 1918);

Jessie Penn-Lewis, *The Magna Charta of Woman* (Bornemouth, Great Britain: The Overcomer Book Room, 1919);

Jessie Penn-Lewis, *The 'Magna Charta' of Woman According to the Scripture Being Light upon the Subject Gathered from Dr. Katherine Bushnells Book 'God's Word to Women'* (Leicester, Great Britain, 1919);

Katharine Bushnell, *101 Questions Answered: A Women's Catechism – God's Word to Women* (Southport, Great Britain: Lowes Ltd., 1930): pp. 31-54;

Katharine Bushnell, *Was sagt Gott der Frau* (Berlin, 1936);

Katharine Bushnell, *The Badge of Guilt and Shame* (Southport, Great Britain, w.y.);

Paul Petry, "Das verschleierte Haupt: Der Schlüssel zu 1. Korinther 11, 3-15: richtige Teilung und richtige Übersetzung dieses Abschnitts," *Licht und Leben* (Gladbeck/Essen, Germany) 67 (1956): pp. 52-54;

Ernestine von Trott zu Solz, *Die Stellung der Frau nach der Bibel* (Asendorf, Germany: Landheim Salem e. V.): pp. 22-32;

J. C. Hurd, *The Origin of 1Corinthians* (New York: Seabury, 1965): p. 163;

Joyce Harper, *Women and the Gospel,* C. B. R. F. Occasional Paper 5 (Pinner, Great Britain: Christian Brethren Research Fellowship, 1974): pp. 23-28;

Jessie Penn-Lewis, *The Magna Charta of Woman* (Minneapolis: Bethany House Publ., 1975): pp. 35-46;

Ralph Woodrow, *Women's Adornment: What does the Bible Really Say* (Riverside: Ralph Woodrow Evangelistic Association, 1976): pp. 36-49;

Alan Padgett, "Paul on Women in the Church: The Contradictions of Coiffure in 1Corinthians 11.2-16," *Journal for the Study of the New Testament 20* (1984): pp. 69-86;

3. The Alternative View in Detail   43

This interpretation has nothing to do with the historical-critical opinion which, based on the vocabulary, considers 1Co 11:2-16 to either have been composed by someone other than Paul[100] or to be a later interpolation,[101] which should be removed.[102] The alternative interpretation had already been suggested long before the advent of the historical critical method.

The quotation theory of John Lightfoot, a 17th century Hebraicist (1602-1675),[103] has influenced me strongly ever since I be-

---

Alan Padgett, "Authority over Her Head," *Daughters of Sarah 12*, no. 1 (Chicago, 1986): pp. 5-9;

Thomas P. Shoemaker, "Unveiling of Equality: 1Corinthians 11:2-16," *Biblical Theological Bulletin 17* (New York, 1987): pp. 60-63;

Michael Molthagen, *Der Schleier im Christentum*, 10 pp. (2000), www.answering-islam.de/German/schleier/ schleier_nt.pdf (last used 1.3.2002)

[Older articles of myself are:

Thomas Schirrmacher, "Bibelstellen, die Aussagen über die Frau beinhalten," *Gemeinde Konkret Nr. 13* (Erfstadt/Bonn, Germany: IWG, Jan. 1985): pp. 9-10;

Thomas Schirrmacher, "Paulus wider das Kopftuch: Ein alternative Sicht zu 1. Korinther 11,2-16," *Querschnitte 2* (Bonn, Germany: VKW, 1989): p. 2;

Thomas Schirrmacher, "Paulus im Kampf gegen den Schleier. Eine alternative Auslegung von 1.Korinther 11,2-16," *AGORA, Krelinger Studenten Rundbrief Nr. 24* (Feb. 1992): pp. 26-31.]

On the biography of Katharine Bushnell, missionary doctor in China who reached a better protection of women in India, see B. J. MacHaffie. "Bushnell, Kathryn (1856-?)". pp. 203 in: Daniel G. Reid u.a. (ed.), *Dictionary of Christianity in America* (Downers Grove: InterVarsity Press, 1990); "Bushnell, Miss Kate". pp. 141-142 in: Frances E. Willard, Mary A. Livermore (ed.), *A Woman of the Century: Fourteen Hundred-Seventy Biographical Sketches Accompanied by Potraits of Leading American Women in All Walks of Life* New York: Gordon Press, 1975, reprinted from 1893) (with picture of Bushnell).

[100] W. O. Walker, "The Vocabulary of 1Corinthians 11:3-16: Pauline or Nonpauline?" *Journal for the Study of the New Testament 35* (1989): pp. 75-88.

[101] A. Loisy. *Remarques sur la littérature épistolaire du Noveau Testament*. (Paris: Nourry, 1935): pp. 60-62; later, for example: B. G. W. Trompf, "On Attitudes Toward Women in Paul and Paulinist Literature: 1Corinthians 11:3-16 and Its Context," *The Catholic Biblical Quarterly 42* (1980): pp. 196-215; W. O. Walker, "1Corinthians 11:2-16 and Paul's Views Regarding Women," *Journal of Biblical Literature 94* (1975): pp. 94-110; Lammar Cope, "1Corinthians 11:2-16: One Step Further," *Journal of Biblical Literature 97* (1978): pp. 435-436.

[102] Certainly some of the arguments brought in the interpolation theory are significant, in so far as they attempt to explain the inner contradiction in the text.

[103] Alan Padgett, *Paul on Women in the Church*, op. cit., p. 85, n. 17, assumes that the opinion he represents first appeared in "Horae Hebraicae et Talmudicae", but errs in

came familiar with him as a co-author of the well-known Calvinist *Westminter Confession* which best expresses my own personal confession of faith. He was

"Pastor and Vice Chancellor of the University of Cambridge, a great Orientalist whose rabbinical scholarship and enthusiasm for encouraging a better understanding of Scripture through knowledge of the original languages, style, customs and history, the geography and natural history of the Jewish people in the writings of his professors, bore fruit for the exegesis of the Old and New Testaments "[104].

Lightfoot was one of the most important members of the Assembly of Westminster[105] which wrote the Westminster Confession which has strongly influenced both Calvinism and the Reformed Church. His last and best work,[106] a book on Hebrew and Talmudic parallels to selected New Testament books[107] which appeared in 1675, has been considered a standard work on the

---

attributing the work to the patristic scholar, Joseph Barber Lightfoot (1828-1889), Bishop of Durham, probably because he cites a translation and an 1859 edition of John Lightfoot's works which he considers the original. Padgett's interpretation of 1Corinthians 11:10 had actually been introduced by John Lightfoot 200 years earlier, in 1675.

[104] Pressel, "John Lightfoot," *Real-Encyklopädie für protestantische Theologie und Kirche* vol. 8 (ed. J. J. Herzog (Leipzig: J. C. Hinrichs'sche Buchhandlung, 1881): pp. 674-675.

[105] Compare the biography in James Reid. *Memoirs of the Lives and Writings of those Eminent Divines who convened in the Famous Assembly at Westminster in the Seventeenth Century,* vol. 2 (Paisly: S. & A. Young, 1815): pp. 55-70. Reprint: James Reid, *Memoirs of the Lives and Writings of those Eminent Divines* (Edinburgh: Banner of Truth Trust, 1982): pp. 55-70.

[106] Pressel, "Lightfoot," op. cit., p. 675. See also Lukas Vischer's *Die Auslegungsgeschichte von 1Kor 6,1-11: Rechtsverzicht und Schlichtung*, Beiträge zur Geschichte der neutestamentlichen Exegese 1 (Tübingen: J. C. B. Mohr, 1955): p. 88.

[107] John Lightfoot, *Horae hebraicae et talmudicae in Evangelia, Acta Apostolorum, in quaedam capita Epistolae ad Romanos et in Epistolam primam ad Corinthios* (Leipzig, 1675). Reprinted frequently since 1684 with John Lightfoot's collected works (see James Reid, op. cit.). I cite the edition; John Lightfoot. *The whole Writings of the Rev. John Lightfoot ... Volume XII containing Horae Hebraicae et Talmudicae or Hebrew and Talmudical Exercitations upon the Gospels of St. Luke and St. John, upon some few Capters of the Epistle to the Romans and The First Epistle to the Corinthians* (London: J. F. Dove, 1823).

subject, comparable to the modern *Strack-Billerbeck*[108], and was reprinted in 1990.[109]

John Lightfoot demonstrates in great detail that Jewish women, although completely veiled outside the home, were free to lay aside their headcoverings during the church service.[110] His question is whether Paul is supporting or rejecting the adoption of the Jewish custom by Gentile-Christian congregations.[111]

3.2. Argumentation for the 13 Propositions

In the following section I will first discuss or enlarge upon the individual propositions, *treating the first three together.*

Proposition 1

Nowhere does the text define the sort of "custom" it refers to. Only verse 15 mentions a concrete garment, the *"veil"* which in no way resembles the scarf used nowadays. Even if the text is indeed referring to clothing, the garment intended is not a scarf, but a **veil** or a **cape**, as indicated by the expression, *"to have something hanging from the head"* (usually inexactly translated as "having something on the head") and by the Jewish custom of veiling. The question of the extent of the veiling remains unanswered. We do not know whether the veil covered nose and mouth, or as most assume, only the head, as is the case with the "substitute veil", the hair.

Proposition 2

Few of those who insist on the veil for praying women have investigated the exact custom and type of garment intended. They rightly insist that not modern custom, but Biblical commandments should set the standard, and justify the continuing validity of 1Co 11:2-16 for modern Christians. **By applying the modern garment to the text, without investigating the original**

---

[108] Hermann Strack and Paul Billerbeck, *Kommentar zum Neuen Testament aus Talmud und Midrasch.* 6 vols. (Munich: C. H. Beck, 1986).

[109] John Lightfoot, *A Commentary on the New Testament from the Talmud and Hebraica.* 4 vols. (Peabody, Mass.: Hendrickson Publ., 1990).

[110] John Lightfoot who*le Writings ...* Vol. XII, op. cit., pp. 512-514.

[111] Please note that my arguments follow a different path.

custom, they make the same mistake which they criticize in others, that is, interpreting Scripture according to their own culture. I cannot imagine that the Christian champions of the scarf would accept the complete covering which leaves only eyes, nose and mouth open to view for today.

Proposition 3

Few proponents of headcoverings for women have investigated the situation discussed in the text. Is Paul dealing with Communion, prophetesses, church meetings, prayer groups, worship or with everyday life in general? In these matters, they would seem to follow their own cultural norm, an impression reinforced by the description of the supposed customs of the Greeks, Romans or Jews of the day. There is, for example, no proof that Corinthian prostitutes were distinguished by short hair, whereas early Greek, Roman and Jewish men generally wore their hair long. The only convincing evidence is the Jewish custom that the woman was always to be veiled (a custom not however commanded in the Old Testament).

The first three propositions in detail

Various interpretations assert various supposed Greek, Roman or Jewish customs. These statements are either unsubstantiated or are only partly supported by the evidence which is much too varied to definitely verify the customs of any one culture, or to distinguish the custom prevalent in Corinth at the time of 1Co.[112] Gordon Fee,[113] for example, simply claims that men have never worn any headcoverings in any culture, although this statement is contradicted by many examples, some in the Old Testament.[114] Norbert Baumer writes:

---

[112] For a good introduction to archeological finds pertinent to 1Corinthians, see: Jerome Murphy-O-Connor, *St. Paul's Corinth: Texts and Archaeology,* Good News Studies (Wilmington, D.E., 1983).

[113] Gordon D. Fee, *The First Epistle to the Corinthians*, The New International Commentary on the New Testament (Grand Rapids, Minn.: Wm B. Eerdmans, 1987): pp. 507-508.

[114] See Richard Oster, "When Men Wore Veils to Worship," op. cit., p. 505.

"Many Jewish, Oriental and Greek men wore headcoverings because of the heat. Did they remove their headcloths before worship?"[115]

The complete covering of men is, however, not common in the world. The only people whose men veil themselves totally are the Tuareg of the Sahara in North Africa.[116]

The case is similar with the common claim that short hair was the sign of the prostitute. There are examples of long-haired temple prostitutes. William J. Martin writes:

"There does not seem to be enough evidence in the works of secular writers to suggest that 'short hair' was the mark of a prostitute."[117]

Gordon Fee has studied the commentaries which consider short hair the emblem of the prostitute, and has observed that they refer only to each other, but never offer any real evidence.[118] Besides, the New Testament itself mentions one long-haired harlot (Lk 7:36-50).[119] Many interpretations discuss the Jewish or Roman hair styles common in Corinth, but generally ignore the extensive archaeological finds in Corinth.

Cynthia L. Thompson[120] has studied the busts of the period and concludes that, whereas the men usually wore their hair short,

---

[115] Norber Baumert, *Antifeminismus bei Paulus?,* op. cit., p. 61.

[116] "The Tuareg are the only people in the world whose men wear a veil over the face, the *Litham*, an indigo blue cloth which they never remove in public." (Volker Panzer. "Sahara – ein verlorenes Paradies: Zum Ursprung der Wüstenvölker", *Terra X: Von Atlantis zum Dach der Welt,* ed. by Gottfried Kirchner (Bergisch-Gladbach, Germany: Gustav Lübbe Verlag, 1988): p. 107. "The modern Tuareg have no explanation. They find it simply decent ..." (ibid. with illustration, p. 108).

[117] William J. Martin, "1 Corinthians 11:2-16," op. cit., p. 233, note 4. See also Gordon Fee, *The First Epistle to the Corinthians,* op. cit., p. 511, note 80.

[118] Ibid.

[119] See Werner de Boor, *Der Erste Brief des Paulus an die Korinther,* Wuppertaler Studienbibel (Wuppertal, Germany: Brockhaus, 1983): p. 181, note 3.

[120] Cynthia L. Thompson, "Hairstyles, Head-coverings and St. Paul: Portraits from Roman Corinth," *Biblical Archaeologist 51* (1988): pp. 99-115, (further literature on pages 113-115).

there were significant exceptions.[121] Many philosophers, priests and foreign workers wore their hair long, partly to demonstrate their subservience.

In Pre-Christian Greece, men, women and children wore long hair.[122] Later, men began to wear it shorter. During the period of the Persian wars, double braids were popular for men[123] and at times, men's hairstyles could not be distinguished from women's.[124] Slaves had short hair[125] but in the fifth century B.C. only female slaves did, since the short hair of the athletes had become the ideal. Men's male hairstyles later became longer in imitation of Alexander the Great.[126]

The early Romans wore their hair long until the time of Alexander the Great.[127] By the time of Augustus, long hair had again become popular among the nobility.[128] The Romans also covered their heads at sacrifices and during worship rituals.[129]

Ernst Lerle has proven that ancient peoples wore veils not as a sign of subservience, but of liberty and honor.[130]

The Talmudic view presented above must therefore be seen as relative. The veil seems to have been general practice for women, although we are not yet certain when the custom arose. This is not

---

[121] These exceptions lead her to object to Paul's supposed argument, "nature teaches you". Ibid., p. 104.

[122] Walter Hatto Groß, "Haartracht. Haarschmuck" in *Der kleine Pauly: Lexikon der Antike*, vol 2., ed. Konrat Ziegler, Walter Sontheimer (Munich: dtv, 1979): column 897-899, p. 897. See also Bremer, "Haartracht und Haarschmuck: A. Griechenland" in *Paulsy Realencyclopädie der Classischen Altertumswissenschaft*, ed. Georg Wissowa (Stuttgart, Germany: J. B. Methler, 1912): col. 2112-2118.

[123] Ibid., col. 2117.

[124] Ibid., col. 2125-2128 .

[125] Walter Hatto Groß, "Haartracht, Haarschmuck," op. cit., p. 897.

[126] Ibid., pp. 897-898.

[127] Steiniger, "Haartracht und Haarschmuck: B. Rom" in *Paulsy Realencyclopädie der Classischen Altertumswissenschaft*, ed. Georg Wissowa (Stuttgart, Germany: J. B. Methler, 1912): col. 2135-2150.

[128] Walter Hatto Groß, op. cit., p. 898.

[129] R. E. Oster, "When Men Wore Veils to Worship," op. cit., pp. 488-505.

[130] Ernst Lerle, *Eine Macht auf dem Haupte?* (Uelzen, Germany: Lutheraner Verlag, nd.): pp. 6-16.

the case for the male headcovering. When a proponent of the quotation theory writes that the man

"had to wear the Jewish *talith*, a veil, not a scarf, as a sign of his guilt and damnation"[131],

one must add that the sources indicate that this was general practice but originally not obligatory.[132] Not until the fourth century does the custom seem to have become general practice, still later to have become mandatory.[133] This was not yet the case in Paul's day.

Besides, the priest's headcovering was considered a symbol of his dignity. Ernst Lerle writes:

"The priest's official habit included a special headcovering as an emblem of his dignity. ... Ex 38:40b: "for glory and beauty."[134]

The cultures of the peoples concerned thus indicate no specific custom, hairstyle or garment which would apply to this text. This is problematic for those who see a generally valid commandment in 1Co 11:2-16. How can one command behavior without knowing exactly what the commandment involves?

The confusion over the Greek terminology makes things more difficult still. M. Latke summarizes the two problems: "It is still unclear which headcovering Paul means, the origin of the custom he is referring to, that is, what Paul is actually criticizing."[135]

The bouquet of interpretations above shows the significance of the question of the specific hairstyle and garment intended by the Greek terms. We cannot afford to ignore the problem or act as if

---

[131] Paul Petry, "Das verschleierte Haupt: Der Schlüssel zu 1. Korinther 11,3-16: richtige Teilung und richtige Übersetzung dieses Abschnitts," *Licht und Leben 67* (Gladbeck/Essen, 1956): p. 53.

[132] Paul Billerbeck, *Die Briefe des Neuen Testaments und der Offenbarung Johannis, Kommentar zum Neuen Testament aus Talmud und Midrasch* (Munich: C. H. Beck, 1979): pp. 423-424.

[133] Ibid., pp. 425-426.

[134] Ernst Lerle, *Eine Macht auf dem Haupte?*, op. cit., p. 10 (note 20). See also Ezekiel 44:20 (Paul Billerbeck, *Die Briefe des Neuen Testaments*, op. cit., pp. 440-441).

[135] M. Lattke, *"kephale* Kopf, (Ober-)Haupt," *Exegetisches Wörterbuch zum Neuen Testament*, vol. 2, ed. Horst Balz, Gerhard Schneider (Stuttgart: W. Kohlhammer, 1981): col. 701-708. (See columns 701-703 for further literature).

the text is definitely referring to a specific garment. The discussion must deal with the expressions, "To have something on the head" in verse 4, "covered" in verses 5-7 and 13 and "Veil" in verse 15.

This last term can, in my opinion, hardly be anything other than a veil.[136] *"Periballaion"* designates more than a headscarf; it is a cape, a cloak or a mantle.[137] The Greek translation of the Old Testament, the *Septuaginta*, uses the term in the same way,[138] as in Dt 22:12, Isa 50:3 and 59:17; Eze 16:13 and 27:7. **Heb 1:12** used this term in its quotation of Ps 102:27 (*LXX* Ps 101:27) which speaks of God *folding the world up "like a cloak".*

The case is similar with the term *"covered"* (verses 6-7, Greek *"kakakalypto"*). The *Septuaginta* uses the term to describes the angels covering their faces in God's presence (Isa 6:2) or the veil which hid the Ark of the Covenant from view (Ex 26:34).[139]

All there is left to discuss is whether the required garment covered the whole face or not.[140] Cynthia Thompson assumes on the basis of her examination of Corinthian busts and of Oriental and Mediterranean examples that the veil did not cover the nose and mouth.[141] Christian Wolf believes that the covering referred not to a veil, but to a mantle drawn over the head[142] which would have the same result.

---

[136] See Ernst Lerle, op. cit., pp. 6-7.

[137] Walter Bauer, Kurt and Barbara Aland, *Wörterbuch zum Neuen Testament* (Berlin: Walter de Gruyter, 1988): col. 1303-1304. See also Walter Bauer, Kurt and Barbara Aland, *Wörterbuch zum Neuen Testament*, Walter de Gruyter (Berlin, 1988) Joseph H. Thayer, *Greek-English Lexicon of the New Testament* (Grand Rapids: Baker Book House, 1977): p. 502, nr. 4016 and 4018. Also Henry Georg Liddel, Robert Scott, *A Greek English Lexicon* (Oxford: At the Clarendon Press, 1940, repr. 1966), 1369-1370.

[138] Joseph H. Thayer, *Greek-English Lexicon of the New Testatment,* op. cit., p. 502, col. 4016 and 4018. See also Walter Bauer, Kurt and Barbara Aland, *Wörterbuch zum Neuen Testament,* op. cit., col 1303-1304.

[139] See Albrech Oepke, *"kalypto, kalymma, anakalypto ...,"* in *Theologisches Wörterbuch zum Neuen Testament*, vol. 3 (Stuttgart: W. Kohlhammer, 1990): p. 563.

[140] Ibid. Othoniel Motta, "The Question of the Unveiled Woman (1Cor. xi,2-16)," *The Expository Times 44* (1933): pp. 139-141, advocates the interpretation that the veil left the face free.

[141] Cynthia L. Thompson, *op. cit.,* p. 113.

[142] Christian Wolff, *op. cit.,* p. 67.

The words "covered" and "uncovered" have such a broad range of meanings that they cannot clarify the matter sufficiently. Leroy Birney sees evidence in the difference between 2Co 3:18 (uncovered face), Mose's veil in 2Co 3:13 and the covering of the head in 1Co 11 that our text requires only the covering of the hair.[143]

An examination of the original text contradicts this view, however, for Paul uses the same root , "kalymma" or "anakalypto", for "veil" and "unveiled" in 2Co 3:13 and 18[144] as for "to veil" in 1Co 11:6-7 (Greek "katakalypto" "to cover"). Since 2Co 3:13-18 refers to the covering of the face,[145] it would seem to indicate that the veil in 1Co 11 covers the face, not only the head.

Of course, 2Co 3 which discusses a figurative, spiritual veiling, to the literal, material covering[146], is not necessarily applicable. Even so, the text uses the imagery of the covered face to imply that the Jews are blind. If this means that 1Co 11 requires the covering of the head , but not the face, then 2Co 3 might as well mean that the face is covered, but not the head. *Besides, 2Co 3 says cleary that all believers, women as well as men, may come before God with uncovered faces:*

"But we all, with unveiled face, beholding as in a mirror the glory of the Lord, are being transformed into the same image from glory to glory, just as by the Spirit of the Lor)." (2Co 3,18)

---

[143] Leroy Birney, "The Role of Women in the New Testament Church," *Christian Brethren Review 33* (Exeter: Paternoster, Dec. 1983): pp. 15-32. See the refutation by Mary Evans, "A Response to L. Birney's 'The Role of Women in the New Testament Church,'" in the same journal, pp. 33-40.

[144] See Archibald Thomas Robertson, *Word Pictures in the New Testament*, vol. 4, *The Epistles of Paul* (1931, repr. Grand Rapids, MI.: Baker Book House, n.d.): p. 159. The common meaning of the terms is most clearly described in Albrecht Oepke, *"kalypto, kalymman, anakalypto ...,"* op. cit.

[145] F. W. Grosheide, *De Tweede Breif aan de Kerk te Korinthe, Commentaar op het Nieuwe Testament* (Kampen, Netherlands: J. H. Kok, 1959): pp. 110-111.

[146] Paul speaks figuratively here, using a concrete example from Ex 34. This view is contradicted, for example, by Samuel Krauss, "The Jewish Rite of Covering the Head", *op. cit.,* p. 136. Krauss sees no indication in 2Co 3 that Jewish men prayed with their heads covered. On Ex 34:29-33, see P. Cürlis, *Der zweite erhaltene Brief Pauli an die Korinther* in *70 Stunden ausgelegt für Gemeinde und Gemeinschaft* (Neumünster, Germany: G. Ihloff, 1928): pp. 151-152.

1Co 11:4 is essential to the discussion of the extent of the headcovering. The translation, "to have something on the head" is an interpretation in itself, and is unacceptable as evidence.[147] As the term means, "to have something hanging from the head",[148] many exegetes believe that long hair is meant.[149] If we assume, however, that a garment is meant, it must be one that hangs from the head, either a veil, or a sort of mantilla which left the face free, or a mantle drawn over the head.

Excursus: The Jewish Custom of Veiling Women

The Talmud which was collected by Jewish Rabbis,[150] contains texts which speak very positively of women,[151] *as well as a number which do not agree with the Old Testament.* (Let me emphasize that I do not wish to discredit Judaism. I also know that the State of Israel requires women to do military duty, although that is one of the last areas in which even feminists recognize a difference between men and women.) The ten curses cast on Eve, according to the Talmud, play a central role.[152] One of these curses commands the complete veiling of the women outside of the house: *"She shall be covered like a mourner"* and *"She shall not be seen with bared head"*[153] The Babylonian Talmud intro-

---

[147] Jerome Murphy-O'Connor, "1Corinthians 11:2-16 Once Again," *op. cit.*, pp. 267-268, goes into detail. See also Jerome Murphy-O'Connor, "Sex and Logic in 1Corinthians 11:2-16 ," *op. cit.*, pp. 483-484; and Alan Padgett, "Paul on Women in the Church," *op. cit.*, p. 70.

[148] *'kata kefales echon':* 'kata'='down', 'kefales'='head', 'echon'='having'. See also James B. Hurley, "Did Paul Require Veils or Silence of Women?" *op. cit.*, pp. 195-200; Jerome Murphy-O'Connor, *1Corinthians, New Testament Message 10* (Wilmington, DE,: M. Glazier, 1979): pp. 103-109. (He believes the text can only refer to the hair, not to a garment, but proffers no good evidence for his opinion.).

[149] See James B. Hurley and other proponents of this interpretation in 2.2 above.

[150] The best Protestant criticism of the Talmud is Gary North's *The Judeo-Christian Tradition,* (Tyler, Texas: Institute for Christian Economics, 1990).

[151] Interestingly enough, these texts have only been compiled by Reinhold Mayer, *Der Talmud* (Munich: Wilhem Goldmann Verlag, 1981). See the Index.

[152] *Encyclopedia Judaica*, vol. Di-Fo (Jerusalem, 1971), s. v. "Eve". Katharine Bushnell, op. cit., p. 12.

[153] Summarized by Katharine Bushnell, *Was sagt Gott der Frau* (Berlin, 1936): p. 51. See the discussion of the Talmud's teaching on women's headcoverings by the Jewish researcher Samuel Krauss, "The Jewish Rite of Covering the Head", *Hebrew Union*

duces the theme of veiling in its commentary on Ge 3. The standard work on the Talmudic parallels to the New Testament says about 1Co 11:2-16:

"The Halaka forbade the Jewish woman to leave the house with bared head. To leave the house with her head uncovered was considered unchaste and adequate grounds for divorce.[154] Besides head coverings, our sources mention a veiling or covering of the woman's face. The ten curses which God is said to have pronounced on Eve, included the command that she should be veiled like a mourner which indicates that she was to hide her face down to the mouth ... How strictly a decent woman was expected to keep this law can be seen in the expectation that not even the husband's closest relatives were supposed to recognize her features."[155]

It is, therefore, worthwhile to read this section of the Talmud in the light of 1Co 11:2-16, even though it is initially difficult to understand its logic.

„Ten curses were cast upon Hava[156]; it is said: *To the woman, He said: I will increase*, that is the two bleedings, the menstrual bleeding and the virginal bleeding; *your labor*, that is the torment of raising children; *your pregnancy*, that is the torment of pregnancy; *in pain shall you bear children*, according to the reading, *your desire shall be for your husband*, this teaches that the wife will desire her husband, when he is on a journey; but *he shall rule over you*, this teaches that the woman desires with her heart, but the man with the lips. This

---

College Annual, UCA 19 (1945-46): pp. 254-163. (On the non-covering of the man, see the same source, pp. 135-154).

[154] This is apparently the source of Christian Briem's and David Goodings opinion that removing the headcovering is just as shameful as adultery. (More detailed indications in Paul Billerbeck, *Die Briefe des Neuen Testaments und der Offenbarung Johannis, Kommentar zum Neuen Testament aus Talmud und Midrasch* (Munich: C. H. Beck, 1979): pp. 427, 429-430. Divorce due to failure to cover the head was justified by interpreting the word 'uncleanness' in Dt 24:1 to mean 'baring the head', Ibid., p. 429, section b. On divorce because of not covering the head, see Ernst Lerle. *Eine Macht auf dem Haupte?* (Uelzen, Lutheraner-Verlag), pp. 14-15.

[155] Paul Billerbeck, op. cit., pp. 429-434.

[156] 'Hava' = Eve.

is only a desirable moral for the wife? – We believe that she must flatter him. These are only seven? [out of ten curses. Author's note]. When R. Dimi came, he explained: She goes veiled, as one afflicted; she is separated from her husband, and is confined in a prison [in her home. Author's note]. – Why is she separated from her husband; would one say, because she may not be alone [with men], so may the husband also not be alone [with women]!? No, this indicates that intercourse with two [men] is forbidden. It is taught in a Berajtha: she has her hair washed like Lilith, she kneels and urinates like an animal, and she serves the man as a cushion. – and he? – He is to be praised, for R. Hija says: It is said: *he teaches us by the beasts of the field, and by the birds of heaven does he give us wisdom; he teaches us by the beasts*, that is the mule, that kneels and urinates; *he gives us wisdom by the birds of heaven*, that is the rooster, that first caresses (the hen) and afterwards copulates with her."[157]

Did Paul share the Jewish attitude towards women, in particular the Jewish-Middle Eastern custom of veiling and the prohibition of cutting the hair, and wish to make it binding on all people? Is the veil, as we know it in many parts of the Islamic world[158], the fulfillment of Biblical order-even if it is only worn during the church service? It would seem that Paul was opposing Grecian and Roman customs by referring to Jewish rules (not, however, to the Old Testament!). Hans Conzelmann asks, for example, if Paul intends to make Jewish decorum obligatory for all Christians, as Werner Kümmel has suggested. [159] Gordon Fee also believes that Paul is arguing in 1Co 11:2-16 in reference to Jewish custom.[160] Conzelmann writes,

---

[157] Translated from German.

[158] The Islamic custom of veiling women did not originate directly from Mohammed and the Koran, but was established later, together with other rules of dress.

[159] Hans Conzelmann, "Der erste Brief an die Korinther", *Kritisch-exegetische Kommentar über das Neue Testament 5,* (1981): p. 225 (includes further material on Jewish custom).

[160] Gordon D. Fee, *The First Epistle to the Corinthians*, p. 33.

„The Jewish custom can be clearly determined, and it agrees with Paul's regulation: the Jewish woman could only appear in public with her head covered."[161] In the course of our discussion of the various propositions, we will see that there are many other serious arguments that suggest that Paul was indeed recommending the veil, as long as one ignores the alternative interpretation. Many theologians, therefore, are only concerned with the question of the veiling of the woman[162] in the New Testament[163] that is.

The Church Father Quintus Septimus Florens **Tertullian** understood the Scriptures this way. In his work *"De virginibus velandis"*[164] ("On the veiled virgins"), he refers to 1Co 11:2-16 in order to propagate the veiling of the woman outside of the

---

[161] Hans Conzelmann, op. cit., p. 225.

[162] See Werner Foerster in *Theologisches Wörterbuch zum Neuen Testament*, vol. 2, ed. by Gerhard Kittel, op. cit., s. v. *in "exestin, exousia ..."*, p. 559-570. See also Heinrich Schlier, Ibid., vol. 3, p. 678, s. v. *"kephale, anakephalaioomai"*.

[163] Albrecht Oepke, Ibid., p. 563, s. v. *"kalypto, kalymma, anakalypto ..."*.

[164] 'De virginibus velandis', especially the last section XVII; Latin Original: Q. S. Fl. Tertulliani, *De Virginibus Velandis* (ed. by E. Dekkers), p. 1209-1226 in: Quinti Septimi Florentis, Tertulliani Opera. Pars II Opera Montanistice, Corpus Christianorum Series Latina II, II. (Brepols: Turnholti, 1954) (with an explicit reference to 1Co 11 in Chapter IV, VII, VIII, XI, XVII, pp. 1212, 1216, 1218, 120 and 1226. See the Latin text with German translation and an excellent introduction in the dissertation (Basel) of Christoph Stücklin, *Tertulian: De Virginibus Velandis* (Bern: H. Lang, 1974).This work was written by the later montanistic Tertullian. But Tertullian represented this view also in his catholic period earlier, just a little bit more gentle. See 'De Oratione', in Q. S. Fl. Tertulliani, *De Oratione* (ed. by F. Diercks): pp. 255-274, in Quinti Septimi Florentis, Tertullian Opera, Pars I., Corpus Christianorum Series Latina II, I. (Brepols: Turnholti, 1954) or together with 'De virginibis velandis' in Gerardus Frederik Dierks (ed.), Q. S. Fl. Tertullianus, *De oratione et De virginbus velandis libelli, Stromata patrisica et mediae valia* 4 (Ultraiecti: Spectrum, 1956). A German translation can be found in: 'Über das Gebet' in K. A. Heinrich Keller (ed.), *Tertullians private und katechetische Schriften,* vol. 1 of *Bibliothek der Kirchenväter: Tertullians ausgewählte Schriften in Deutsche übersetzt* (Kempten/Munich: Kösel, 1912): pp. 247-273, here pp. 263-268. For more references see Gösta Claeson, *Index Tertullianeus*, vol. 3 Q-Z (Paris: Études Augustiniennes, 1975): pp. 1707-1708. The best insight into Tertullians view of woman is: 'Über den weltlichen Putz', K. A. Heinrich Keller (ed.), *Tertullians ... Schrifen*, op. cit., pp. 175-202, a condensation on pp. 175-176. See also a survey of this topic by Otto Bardenhewer, *Patrologie* (Freiburg: Herder, 1910³): pp. 162-164.

home[165], a view which apparently won no acceptance in the rest of the Church. He teaches a very extensive veiling:

"The situation of the second century is very clear, for Tertullian disapproved of women who veiled themselves only insufficiently, and criticized those who covered their forehead, but left their heads or their ears free. He admonished the women to cover the whole head and demanded that they wear a veil as long as their unbound hair."[166]

Tertullian disagreed with other Church Fathers in this matter. The Early Church was familiar with the veil, but only for consecrated virgins, i.e. for nuns.[167] Only Chrysostomus suggested that 1Co 11:2-16 requires veiling for all women,[168] but, as with Terullian, he recommended not a headscarf, but a complete veil.

Even Adolf Schlatter who takes it for granted that Paul means a scarf and not a veil,[169] assumes that Paul based his directions on Jewish custom[170]. The opinion that Paul was making Jewish custom obligatory for all Christians is wide spread.[171]

---

[165] Tertullian is here only concerned with the question of whether the single woman should be veiled. He assumed that this was automatically the case with married women.

[166] Ernst Lerle, *Eine Macht auf dem Haupte?*, op. cit., p. 6.

[167] Albrecht Oepke, op. cit., p. 565. Compare the mention of veiled nuns in contrast to other women in many papal letters over the centuries: *Die Briefe der Päpste und die an sie gerichteten Schreiben: Von Linius bis Pelagious II. (vom Jahre 67-590). Bibliothek der Kirchenväter*. 7 Volumes (Kempten: Jos. Kösel, 1875-1880).

[168] Chrysostomos, "26th Homilie zum 1. Korintherbrief", in "Ausgewählte Schriften des heiligen Chrysostomos", vol. 5 of *Bibliothek der Kirchenväter*, op. cit., pp. 434-451.

[169] Adolf Schlatter, *Paulus, der Bote Gottes: Eine Deutung seiner Briefe an die Korinther* (Stuttgart: Calwer Verlag, 1969): pp. 308-309. The Puritans wrote similarly, giving no justification, in the seventeenth century. See for example, Matthew Poole, *Commentary on the whole Bible*, vol. 3 (Edinburgh: The Banner of Truth Trust, 1990): p. 577, or Matthew Henry's *Commentary on the whole Bible*, vol. 6 (Iowa Falls: World Bible Publ., USA, 1990), p. 562. In opposition to Schlatter and the frontally open veil, see Ernst Lerle, op. cit., pp. 6-7.

[170] Adolf Schlatter, Ibid., pp. 308-315. See also Adolf Schlatter, "Die korinthische Theologie", *Beiträge zur Förderung christlicher Theologie 18* (Gütersloh: Bertelsmann, 1914): p. 22. Adolf Schlatter, "Die Korintherbriefe", *Erläuterungen zum Neuen Testament 6,* (Stuttgart: Calwer Verlag, 1987): p. 135.

[171] See also Normann Hillyer. "Der erste und zweite Brief an die Korinther", in vol. 4 of *Brockhaus Kommentar zur Bibel*, ed. by Donald Guthrie, J. Alec Motyer (Wupper-

The identification of Scriptural teaching with Talmudic discrimination against the woman has led historical-critical theologians to disregard Paul on the questions of women, marriage and the family. In 1931, Gerhard Delling, for example, discussed Paul's attitude toward the woman and marriage under the headings, "Antipathy Towards Marriage"[172] and "Antipathy towards Women"[173], whereby the "Veil Question"[174] played a major role. The efforts of other historical-critical writers do little to save the apostle's honor and seem rather strained. C. Butler suggests that Paul's discriminatory reputation was due to the mistaken ascription of the pastoral letters to him.[175]

Proposition 4

The only verse (vs 15) which specifically mentions a veil states clearly, "Her hair is given to her for a covering." Whether or not Paul has been arguing for or against the veil, this direction clearly opposes it. If verses 2-14 indicate that a veil is necessary, Paul here says that the women already has one; if the preceding verses were against the use of the veil, verse 15 offers a further argument.

The proposition in detail

The expression 'instead of' (Gr. *'anti'*) which indicates substitution,[176] means that a woman's hair is a substitute for the veil.[177] If Paul had been arguing for any sort of veil, he here concludes that Nature has already provided the woman with one, leaving the question open as to whether hair in general suffices or whether it must

---

tal: Brockhaus Verlag, 1985): p. 326. Werner de Boor, *Der erste Brief des Paulus an die Korinther, Wuppertaler Studienbibel* (Wuppertal: R. Brockhaus, 1983): p. 179.

[172] Gerhard Delling, *Paulus' Stellung zu Frau und Ehe* (Stuttgart: W. Kohlhammer, 1931), pp. 57-95.

[173] Ibid., pp. 96-119.

[174] Ibid., pp. 96-104.

[175] C. Butler, *Was Paul a Male Chauvinist?*, New Blackfriars, no. 659, 56 (1975): pp. 174-179.

[176] Gordon D. Fee. *The First Epistle to the Corinthians*, op. cit., p. 528. On page 529, Fee interprets *'anti'* to mean 'one term pertains to the other'.

[177] The translation 'to be used as' appears nowhere else in Scripture, and is thus not acceptable. See: Alan Padgett, "Paul on Women in the Church," op. cit., pp. 82-83.

be long and hang down. Even if the reader rejects the quotation theory, he may not ignore verse 15; the argument that the woman's hair being a veil makes a supplementary veil necessary is simply not convincing.

The translation of verse 15, *"The hair is given instead of a veil"* which refers to all, instead of *"The hair is given to her as a veil"* will be substantiated in the following proposition.

If, however, Paul is opposing the veil, as we assume, this statement is a further argument. Since God has given human beings hair, why should they require a further covering?!

Proposition 5

The final verse (vs 16) confirms this. "We have no such custom". This custom is not the contention referred to which was common in Corinth, and which Paul has already condemned twice as sin, not as merely exceptional. The 'custom' can only be the veiling discussed in the preceding verses, a custom which we cannot define more definitely. **The Corinthians had a rule unfamiliar to other churches. If Paul rejects the custom, we need not know more about it.** The text states simply that no church can make its own private usage binding on others.

The proposition in detail

Christian Wolff concludes that to consider contention a bad custom "would be too innocuous."[178] The word 'custom' (Gr. *'synetheia'*) designates a habit or tradition.[179] Jn 18:39 employs the same term to describe the Roman custom of freeing a prisoner on Passover. In 1Co 8:7 Paul uses it to designate being accustomed to idolatry.[180] (The interpretation that contention is the 'custom' arises from the assumption that Paul would call some-

---

[178] Christian Wolff, *Der erste Brief des Paulus and die Korinther*, Part 2, op. cit., p. 76.

[179] In the Papyrus as well. See James Hope Moulton and George Milligan, *The Vocabulary of the Greek Testament Illustrated from the Papyri and Other Non-Literary Sources* (1930, repr. Grand Rapids, Mich.: Wm B. Eerdmans, 1985): p. 604.

[180] These are the only uses of the term in the New Testament. In other texts, it can mean 'intimate contact', 'familiarity', Walter Bauer, Kurt and Barbara Aland, *Wörterbuch zum Neuen Testament*, col. 1574; Joseph H. Thayer, *Greek-English Lexicon of the New Testament,* op. cit., p. 604.

thing wrongly disregarded a 'custom'.)[181] The definition of the term 'custom' is of course insufficient to refute the opinion that Paul is opposed to women praying uncovered, but it seems to me that a custom is more likely to be something one does rather than something one omits. The fact that so many translations add footnotes to explain that the custom refers to praying unveiled, suggests that the interpretation is not so obvious that a custom not existing in the church is something that one does *not* do.

Proposition 6

Verses 13-14 are usually rendered as three rhetorical questions, although the original employs no question marks. Since questions in Greek can only be distinguished by interrogatives (such as 'where' or 'how', etc.) or by context, **the questions in these verses could equally well be statements:** *"Judge for yourselves. It is proper for a woman to pray uncovered! Nor does Nature teach you that it is dishonorable for a man to have* (long) *hair, but for a woman an honor to have* (long) *hair!"* The second sentence even must be a statement, because the word *'oude'* never introduces a question. In this case Nature is not used as an argument for a Divine commandment; rather, it becomes clear that Nature cannot be referred to as a source of Divine commandments which can only be derived from the Word of God.

The proposition in detail

Since the word for 'hair' ('koman') usually – but not always – describes long hair, whether it is worn bound or not,[182] the addition 'long' can be set in brackets in the translation. *If the text consists of rhetorical questions, then 'koman' must be translated as 'long hair'. Otherwise Paul would be condemning men with hair!* Interpreters never explain why 'koman' must mean 'long hair' here. The alternative interpretation does not depend on the word meaning either 'hair' in general or specifically 'long hair'.

---

[181] Charles Hodge, *A Commentary on 1 & 2Corinthians* (1857,1859 & 1974, repr. Edinburgh: Banner of Truth Trust, 1988) p. 214.

[182] Cynthia Thompson, "Hairstyles, Head-coverings and St. Paul," op. cit., p. 112.

The subject 'kome' by itself generally means 'hair', but the cognate verb *'komao'* means 'to wear long hair' or 'to let the hair grow long'.[183] The term emphasizes the styling of the hair, not its length.

According to Heinrich Schmidt, 'phobe' means "the long, flowing hair", 'chaite' "loose, falling long hair," 'thrix' "a long quantity of hair falling from the head over the neck". Therefore, 'kome' does not necessarily mean "long hair", since other terms, particularly 'chaite', were available for this designation. Schmidt believes that 'kome' only indicates long hair in that short hair cannot be arranged in a decorative fashion which is the term's basic meaning, since it is derived from the same stem as *'kosmos'*, ("decoration"). He concludes "that *kome* describes the hair as human adornment which indicates length, but that the word does not mean 'long hair'." [184] As the

---

[183] Walter Bauer, Kurt and Barbara Aland, *Wörterbuch zum Neuen Testament*, op. cit., col. 899; Johannes Louw, Eugene A. Nida, ed., *Greek-English Lexicon of the New Testament Based on Semantic Domains* (New York: United Bible Societies, 1989): pp. 96 and 527 *('kome'* and *'komao')*; James Hope Moulton, George Millgan, *The Vocabulary of the Greek New Testament Illustrated from the Papyri and Other Non-Literary Sources*, op. cit., p. 353 *('komao')*; J. N. O'Sullivan, *"kom(ao),"* Lexikon des frühgriechischen Epos*, vol. 2, ed. by Bruno Snell a.o. (Göttingen, Germany: Vandenheock und Ruprecht, 1991): col. 1478; Bremer, "Haartracht und Haarschmuck: A. Griechenland," *Paulys Realencycolpädie der Classischen Altertumswissenschaft*, vol. 14, ed. Georg Wissowa (Stuttgart, Germany: J. B. Metz, 1912): col. 2109-2135 (In the 5th century, *'komao'* was used only for knights and described thick, curly hair.); Henrico Stephano, *Thesaurus Graecae Linguae*, vol. 5 (1829, repr. Graz, Switzerland: Akademische Druck- und Verlagsanstalt, 1954): col. 1772-1776; Fransciscus Zorell, *Lexicon Graecum Novi Testamenti* (Paris: Lethielleux, 1931): col. 724; Carolo Ludov. Willbaldo Grimm, *Lexicon Graeco-Latinum in Libros Novi Testamenti* (Leipzig, Germany: Libraria Arnoldiana, 1888): p. 241+246; S. C. Schirlitz, *Griechisch-Deutsches Wörterbuch* (Giessen, Germany: Ferber, 1851): pp. 1500-1501; Henry Georg Liddel, Robert Scott, *A Greek English Lexicon* (1940, repr. Oxford: At the Clarendon Press, 1966): p. 975; Pierre Chantraine, *Dictionnaire Étymologique de la Langue Grecque: Histoire des Mots;* vol. 1 (Paris: Éditions Lincksieck, 1968): p. 560; Hjalmar Firsch, *Griechisches Ethymoloigsches Wörterbuch* (Heidelberg, Germany: Carl Winter Universtiätsverlag, 1960): pp. 908-909 (*'komao'* = 'to wear long hair' and be resplendent with well-kept hair). The same still applies in modern Greek: G. Giannakomoulou, *Ariston Ellenogermaikon Lexikon*, vol. A, (Michigan: Michigan Press; Athens: P. Koutsoumopos, 1972): p. 631.

[184] Heinrich Schmidt, *Synonymik der griechischen Sprache*, vol. 1 (Leipzig: B. G. Teubner, 1876): pp. 379-388, (repr. Amsterdam: Adolf M Kakkert, 1967).

related verb emphasizes length more strongly, 'kome' may indeed mean 'long hair' in 1Co 11:13-14.[185]

Gordon Fee objects to the translation of verses 13 and 14 as a statement instead of as a question, because it fails to do justice to the expression *'prepon estin'* ('it is proper'),[186] which however is generally used in statements. Mt 3:15 and Heb 2:10, the only other New Testament uses,[187] are also statements.[188] *'Prepon estin'* does not refute the *possibility* that Paul is making a statement rather than asking a question.

In his review of this book, Karl-Heinz Vanheiden comments that it is „formally possible"[189] to translate these verses as statements rather than as questions, but points out that no known translation and no scientific New Testament do so. Besides, such an interpretation presupposes the quotation theory. If, however, it is formally possible to render these verses as statements rather than as questions, the idea should be discussed. Neither the translations nor the punctuation are infallible, for they are interpretations and do not belong to the original text. Many scriptures have been given excellent interpretations not found in translations.

Roland Gebauer also writes in his review:

"Schirrmacher's interpretation of verses 15b+16 is possible, but definitely not unequivocal. His interpretation of verses 13-15a as statements is also conceivable."[190]

---

[185] I have dealt with the term in such detail, because the traditional interpretation of our text is often so inexact and assumes the meaning 'long hair' without having investigated the term.

[186] Gordon D. Fee, *The First Epistle to the Corinthians*, op cit., p. 525, note 4.

[187] Joseph H. Thayer, *Greek-English Lexicon of the New Testament*, op cit., p. 535 (Nr. 4241).

[188] Walter Bauer, Kurt and Barbara Aland, *Wörterbuch zum Neuen Testament*, op. cit., col. 1401.

[189] Karl-Heinz Vanheiden, "Thomas Schirrmacher. Paulus im Kampf gegen den Schleier ...," *Bibel und Gemeinde 99* (1999), p. 38.

[190] Roland Gebauer, "Thomas Schirrmacher. Paulus im Kampf gegen den Schleier ...," *Jahrbuch für evangelikale Theologie 9* (1995), pp. 236-238, here p. 237. Gebauer points out that I refer constantly to others who take the same view – which is one of the usual reasons for footnotes! The criticism that no serious exegete teaches this idea makes such references necessary. Besides, I cannot understand his judgment that

I never asserted that my view is unequivocal, only that Greek grammar permits both interpretatins, and that the decision must depend on the context. The traditional view is not 'unequivocal' either. Why has no one criticised the failure of the commentaries to even mention the problem, much less to discuss it?

Gebauers argument[191] against the translation as statement is actually that Paul's challenge, "Judge for yourselves," makes a question necessary. Does it? The point is that Paul, in speaking of his own judgment, does not intend to give the Corinthians the liberty to decide for themselves; he expects them to accept his decision which he expresses either as a rhetorical question or as a statement.

Vanheiden and Gebauer fail to respond to the grammatical rule that 'oude' is never used in rhetorical questions, either by Paul or in other Greek literature. 'Oude', at the beginning of a sentence means 'not even'. Only the second sentence can be a rhetorical question.

The so named Textus Receptus later added an 'eta' before verse 14 which is usually translated as an interrogative, equivalent to our *"isn't it?"* This would have no value as an argument for the rhetorical question, since 'eta' is generally used with statements and means *"still"* or *"and not"*.

Let me give just one example of a New Testament sentence which can be translated as either question or statement. Jesus' words to Thomas in Jn 20:29 can mean, *"Because you have seen me, have you believed?"*[192], or *"Thomas, because you have seen Me, you have believed."*[193]

The ancient Bohairic and Sahidic translations of the New Testament interpret verse 13-14 as statements, according to Baumert,

"Schirrmacher fails to discuss and prove his proposition on the text itself" (Ibid., p. 238).

[191] Similar Daniel L. Segraves, *Hair Length in the Bible: A Study of ICorinthians 11:2-16*, (Hazelwood: World Aflame Press, 1989), p. 64-65 (first edition 1979 Women's Hair – The Long and Short of It).

[192] *New American Standard.*

[193] *New King James.*

but treat verse 15 as a question.[194] This would indicate that earlier translators were aware that these verses could be understood as rhetorical questions as well as statements. Baumert himself considers verse 11 to be a rhetorical question, verse 14 and 15, however, statements. He writes:

"One ignores a tiny particle in Paul's answer to this objection, reading the opposite meaning into the text. Paul is not asking a question,[195] but is saying, 'Not even Nature teaches you this ...'"[196]

"Verse 14 has caused much perplexity. Why does Nature teach that long hair is shameful for a man? Our foregoing results make this idea increasingly improbable. Why does Paul insists on long hair on women? This would be a new thought, as long hair would be insignificant under a veil. And if long hair is an honor, why must it be covered? Alan Padgett provides a possibility, although he continues in the opposite direction. He correctly notes that Paul never uses *oude* in rhetorical questions. As a matter of fact, this usage is generally unknown in Greek. *Oude* at the beginning of a sentence means 'and not' or 'even when'."[197]

Baumert adds an interesting detail. Whereas most translations render verse 14 as *"Her hair is given **to her** as a covering,"* Baumert excludes the words *"to her"*, as does my translation. The words *"to her"* (Gr. 'aute') is the less preferred reading and should be left out, as it is in the manuscripts p[46], D, F. G and the Majority Text.[198] The text deals therefore not just with the woman's hair serving as a veil or covering, but with all peoples'. Two of Baumert's translations indicate this:[199]

---

[194] Norbert Baumert, *Antifeminismus bei Paulus?,* op. cit., p. 74, note 122.

[195] Baumert adds in note 318: "A question would have begun: *'ou, ouch(i)'. 'Oude'* introduces a statement."

[196] Norbert Baumert, *Frau und Mann bei Paulus*, op. cit., p. 176.

[197] Norbert Baumert, *Antifeminismus bei Paulus*, op. cit., p. 74. Refers to Alan Padgett, "Paul on Women in the Church," op. cit.

[198] Norbert Baumert, *Frau und Mann bei Paulus*, op. cit., p. 176.

[199] We do not share his interpretation completely, as we consider all the verses to be statements and believe that Paul is discussing not the long hair, but a covering.

"Nor does nature itself (of itself) teach you that (a) man (a male), when he lets his hair down (pays attention to it or decorates himself with it), it defaces (or dishonors) him, but (a) woman (a female), when she lets her hair down, it is for her an adornment (ornament, honor); for the hair is given (by Nature to all people) as a covering (protection)."[200]

"Nor does Nature teach you that it is a disgrace (degradation) for a man to let his hair down, but that it is an adornment (honor) for a woman to let her hair down; for the hair is given (to all!) as covering (protection)."[201]

Besides, most interpretations ignore the fact that verses 13 and 14, even as rhetorical questions, can still be answered with "No!", for Paul has challenged his readers "Judge for yourselves!" Must one not answer, "No, Nature does not teach us such things!"?

If one, however, understands verses 13 and 14 as rhetorical questions requiring a positive answer, a dilemma arises. How does Nature instruct us about hair length? As far as I know, no interpreter has yet found a satisfactory answer to this question. Norbert Baumer writes:

"Since the hair of both men and women by nature grows long, one can derive neither a doubt for the man nor a confirmation for the woman."[202]

Not even John Piper and Wayne Grudem who otherwise unquestionably support the traditional view of the woman's role in the New Testament, want to apply the practical implications of the text on headcoverings which they consider culturally relative. They argue:

"How did nature teach that long hair dishonored a man and gave women a covering? Nature has not endowed women with more hair than men."[203]

---

[200] Norbert Baumert, *Antifeminismus bei Paulus*, op. cit., p. 56.

[201] Norbert Baumert, *Frau und Mann bei Paulus*. op. cit., p. 169.

[202] Norbert Baumert, *Antifeminismus bei Paulus*, op. cit., p. 75.

[203] John Piper, Wayne Grudem, ed., *Recovering Biblical Manhood and Womanhood* (Wheaton, Ill.: Crossway Books, 1991): p. 75.

According to Piper and Grudem, Nature teaches only that it is shameful for a man to look like a woman, but that the definition of feminine or masculine appearance depends on custom and culture. This distinction however does no justice to the text which teaches either that hairlength can be derived from Nature, or that Nature has no bearing on the question.

Even a decided advocate of the view that Paul is demanding that women wear a scarf when praying, writes:

"It is not indisputable that Nature teaches it to be shameful for men to wear their hair long."[204]

1Co 11:14 is the only verse in Scripture which uses 'Nature' (Gr. 'Physis') in the nominative case, personifies it or assigns it a normative role,[205] a thought foreign to both the Old Testament and the New, as Helmut Köster has demonstrated in his comparison with Ro 1:18-26 and its view of Nature. Köster sees here the influence of contemporary popular philosophy, particularly of the Stoics, for whom hair style was a "popular *topos* in the discussion of the natural".[206] How could the Corinthian Christians have known what the Stoics taught about hairstyles. or which Stoic opinion Paul meant?

It seems more appropriate to me to assume that Paul is not arguing from Nature, but is refuting the Corinthians' argumentation.

By the way, the church in its history never taught that a man should not wear long hair, like many examples show.

Ever since the Early Church, artists have always portrayed Jesus with long hair hanging down to his shoulders, as the Turin Shroud – whether it is genuine or not – clearly shows.[207] Obvi-

---

[204] William MacDonald, *1Korintherbrief* (Dillenburg, Germany: Emmaus-Fernbibelschule, 1971): p. 119.

[205] Helmut Köhler, *"physis, physikos, physokos"* in *Theologisches Wörterbuch zum Neuen Testament* vol. 9, ed. by Gerhard Kittel (Stuttgart, Germany: W. Kohlhammer, 1990): p. 226.

[206] Ibid., pp. 266-267. See pages 257-260 on the Stoics.

[207] Werner Bulst, (Heinrich Pfeiffer), *Das Turiner Grabtuch und das Christusbild,* vol. I: *Das Grabtuch,* (Frankfurt: Josef Knecht, 1987), pp. 95-127; Heinrich Pfeiffer, (Werner Bulst), *Das Turiner Grabtuch und das Christusbild,* vol. II:. *Das echte Christus-*

ously, the Church has never considered long hair unchristian – otherwise it would have depicted Him differently.

Even very strict Puritan and Congregationalist men in England in the sixteenth to eighteenth centuries, such as Oliver Cromwell, had long hair: only lower class men wore short hair.[208]

Proposition 7

Verses 11-12 which agree with the Scriptural account of Creation, rebut verses 7-8 which contradict it, for Woman was made *"in the image of God"* just as Man was. **The problem is resolved if we assume that verses 4-10 repeat the Corinthian argumentation which Paul then exaggerates.** He used this method frequently in 1 and 2Co (for example in 1Co 6:12-13, 7:1-5, 8:4-7, 10:14-22; 2Co 12:11-15). *"For"* in verse 10 begins Paul's retort; *"nevertheless"* his refutation.

The proposition in detail

Many have noticed the contradiction between the first part of 1Co 11:2-16 and the second.

In verse 7, Man only is *"the image and glory of God"*. Woman is merely *"the glory of man"*. In verse 8, *"man is not from woman, but woman from man"*, but in verse 9, *"Man was not created for the woman, but woman for the man"*.

Verses 11-12, to the contrary, tell us,

"For in the Lord, the woman is not without the man, nor the man without the woman.

For just as the woman comes from man, the man comes from woman; but all things come from God."

Was the woman created *only* for the man or were *both* created for each other? Woman comes from Man (at the Creation), but does not Man come from Woman (at birth)?

Does the difference lie in the expression *"in the Lord"* (verse 11), as some have suggested? What does the expression mean?

---

bild: Das Grabtuch, der Schleier von Manoppello und ihre Wirkungsgeschichte in der Kunst, (Frankfurt: Verlag Josef Knecht, 1991).

[208] Carl N. Degler, "Were the Puritans 'Puritanical?," pp. 45-54 in: Nicholas Cords, Patrick Gerster (Ed.), *Myth and the American Experience* (Champaign, 1989[2]), p. 464.

Do these statements apply only to believers, while those in verses 7-8 apply to all? Why does Paul mention these things at all in verses 11-12 in this context, when they so strongly contradict his argumentation?

Norbert Baumert concludes,
"In verse 11 ff, Paul seems to suddenly correct himself ..."[209]
J. Kürzinger writes, "Few New Testament texts are so dubious in their meaning and so problematic for a convincing translation."[210] He points out that the preposition *"without"* (Gr. 'choris') lacks an object, and translates accordingly, "Besides, neither is Woman different than Man, nor is Man different than Woman in the Lord."[211]
Christian Wolff has rightly recognized the relationship of verses 7-8 to the account of Creation (Ge 1:27) in which God created Man and Woman as His image,
"In his interpretation of Ge 1:27, Paul follows the Jewish exegesis of his day which applied the text only to Adam ..."[212]
He should, however, have noted that this is true only of verses 7-9! Verses 11-12 reflect the Old Testament's position:
"And God said: Let us make people in our image, similar to us! They shall rule over the fish in the sea and over the birds in the air and over the beasts and over the whole earth and over all creeping things that creep on the earth! And God created mankind in his image, in the image of God he created him; as man and woman he created them. And God blessed them, and God said to them, Be fruitful and multiply and fill the earth and make her subject (to you); and rule over the fish of the sea and over the birds of the air and over all animals that move on the earth!" (Ge 1:26-28).

[209] Norbert Baumert, *Antifeminismus bei Paulus?*, op. cit., p. 53.
[210] J. Kürzinger, "Frau und Mann nach 2. Kor. 11:11f," *Biblische Zeitschrift 22* (1978): p. 270.
[211] Ibid., pp. 271-274.
[212] Christian Wolff, *Der erste Brief des Paulus an die Korinther*, Part 2, *Auslegung der Kapitel 8-16, Theologischer Handkommentar zum Neuen Testament* VIII (Berlin: 2. Evangelische Verlagsanstalt, 1982): p. 72.

These verses declare both Man *and* Woman to be the image of God. Both receive the so-called 'cultural commission' to fill the earth – which can only be accomplished by reproduction, by men coming from women – and to *"rule"*.[213]

Hans-Joseph Klauck has attempted to solve the problem by historical-critical source document theory. He believes that the statement made by the so-called priesthood in Ge 1, that Man and Woman are the image of God, was later limited in Ge 2 by the so-called Yahwists.[214] Ge 2, however, as we have already seen, places Woman on the same level as Man who cannot rule over the earth without her.

Other writers have also attempted to resolve the contradiction by applying to the accounts of Creation in Genesis, assuming that Paul first gives the arguments of the classical Jewish interpretation based on Ge 2, and then adds the view of Ge 1 which emphasises the equality of man and woman.[215]

---

[213] Interestingly enough, the theory of evolution which the feminists use to support their views, usually ascribes cultural achievements to Man who supposedly discovered fire, tools etc. Assuming a struggle for survival, the theory of evolution considers the physically stronger Man historically superior to Woman, a view which the Old Testament, based on Creation, never suggests. (See the following text books on the criticism of Feminism: Heide Göttner-Abendroth, *Das Matriarchat* I: *Geschichte seiner Erforschung* (Stuttgart: Kohlhammer, 1989) pp. 16-33.

[214] Hans-Josef Klauck, *Erster Korintherbrief*, op. cit., p. 79. See the refutation by Samuel R. Külling, *Zur Datierung der Genesis-P- Stücke* (Basel, Switzerland: Immanuel Verlag, 1987); R. K. Harrison, *Introduction to the Old Testament* (London: IVP, 1969): pp. 493-662; Gleason L. Archer, *Einleitung in das Alte Testament* vol. 1, (Bad Liebenzell, Germany: Verlag der Liebenzeller Mission, 1987): pp. 97-227. On the alleged contradictory Creation Accounts, see; Thomas Schirrmacher, "Gibt es zwei sich widersprechende Schöpfungsberichte?," *Bibel und Gemeinde 93*, no. 3 (1993): pp. 200-203; Samuel R. Külling, "Sind Genesis 1,1-2,4a und Genesis 2,4b ff zwei verschiedene, widersprüchliche Schöpfungsberichte?," *Bibel und Gemeinde 76* (1976): pp. 217-220; Samuel R. Külling, *Der Schöpfungsbericht und naturwissenschaftliche Fragen* (Riehen: Bibelbund/FETA, 1976); Samuel R. Külling, "Das Verständnis von Gen. 2,4ff und sein Verhältnis zu Gen1,1-2,3, Genesis 13. Teil," *Fundamentum 4* (1983) FETA, pp. 4-16; Samuel R. Külling, "Gibt es zwei Schöpfungsberichte?," *Bibel und Gemeinde 62* (1962): pp. 14-17 and Samuel R. Külling, "Widersprüche in der Bibel?," *Bibel und Gemeinde 65* (1965): pp. 204-306.

[215] L. Ann Jervis, "But I Want to Know: Paul's Midrashic Intertextual Response to the Corinthian Worshipers (1Cor 11:2-16)," *Journal of Biblical Literature 112* (1993), pp. 231-246 and Jason David BeDuhn, "Because of the Angels: Unveiling Paul's Anthropology in 1Corinthians 11," *Journal of Biblical Literature 118* (1999), pp. 295-320.

In **1Co 7:3-4**, Paul has already spoken very clearly about the mutual, not one-sided dependence of Man and Woman: *"Let the husband give his wife what he owes her;* **likewise** *the wife her husband. The wife has no authority over her own body, but her husband;* **likewise** *the husband has no authority over his own body, but his wife."*

In this outline, Thomas P. Shoemaker has shown very clearly how Paul contradicts what has been said before, piece by piece, using the same terms filled or evaluated differently.[216]

The Chiastic Structure of 1Co 11:2-16 according to Thomas P. Shoemaker
A. (2-3) Introduction
B.   (4-7) "woman", "uncovered", "to pray", "man", "glory"
C.   (8a) not "man from woman"
D.   (8b) "woman from man"
E.   (9a) not "man on account of woman"
F.   (9b) "woman on account of man"
(10) For this reason and because of the angels,
Center   the woman ought to have liberty
over her head.
F'   (11a) "Neither the woman apart from man"
E'   (11b) "nor man apart from woman"
D'   (12a) "for just as the woman is from the man"
C'   (12b) "thus also the man is through the woman"
B'   (13-15) "woman", "uncovered", "to pray", "man", "glory"
A' (16) Conclusion

John Lightfoot wrote about this contradiction in 1675,

"But I suppose the apostle looks another way; and ... that he does not here speak in his own sense, but cites something unusual among the Jews."[217]

---

[216] Thomas P. Shoemaker, "Unveiling of Equality: 1Corinthians 11:2-16," *Biblical Theological Bullentin 17* (New York, 1987): pp. 60-63.

He points out that the whole argumentation in verses 4-10 never verifies what it is actually trying to prove.

"For if it were so argued by him [Paul]: Let not a woman pray but with her head covered, because she is subject to her husband; it might be argued in like manner: Let not a man pray but with his head covered, because he is subject to Christ. I fear lest that interpretation which supposeth the veiling of women in this place as a sign of the woman's subjection to her husband should more obscure the sense of this place, obscure enough indeed of itself."[218]

He points out the consequences – which not even the most ardent advocate of a headcovering for praying women would be prepared to accept. If Paul is really demanding a headcovering, then it is first of all a Jewish custom declared universally valid, since the essential nature of Man and Woman is the same universally.

"The obligation of subject towards the husband follows the woman ever and everywhere; ought she ever and everywhere carry a veil with her, as a sign of that subjection?"[219]

To be fair, I must add that the contradiction can be weakened by removing some of the negative connotations from some of the terms. For example, the statement, *"Christ is the head of every Man"* in verse 3 does not necessarily exclude women.

The word used for *'head'* often means not 'ruler', but 'source', a meaning assumed by many interpreters for this text.[220] Also the

---

[217] John Lightfoot, The whole Writings of the Rev. John Lightfoot ... Volume XII containing Horae Hebraicae et Talmuidicae, op.cit., p. 519.

[218] Ibid., p. 515.

[219] Ibid., p. 516.

[220] Z. B. S. Bedale, "The Meaning of kephale in the Pauline Epistles," *Journal of the Theological Society 5* (1954): pp. 211-215; D. Ellul, "?'Sois belle et tais-toi' Est-ce vraiment ce que Paul at dit?: A propos de I Co 11,2-16," *Foi et Vie 88* (Paris, 1989) 5: pp. 49-50; Gordon D. Fee, *The First Epistle to the Corinthians*, op. cit., pp. 502-505; Jerome Murphy-O'Connor, "Sex and Logic in 1Corinthians 11:2-16," op. cit., pp. 492-493; Paul S. Fiddes, "Woman's Head is Man': A Doctrinal Reflection upon a Pauline Text," *The Baptist Quarterly: The Journal of the Baptist Historical Society 31* (London, 1986): pp. 370-383; F. F. Bruce, *1 and 2Corinthian,. in New Centruy Bible Commentary* (1971, repr. Grand Rapids: Wm Eerdmans, 1980): p. 103. Subsequent to Be-

discussion goes back and forth.[221] L. Ann Jervis argues that the word should be translated 'source', because she considers Ge 2 which presents the man as source but not as authority, to be the basis of Paul's arguments.[222] As the meaning of the word 'head' has no special significance in the quotation theory, and because the issue cannot be resolved, I will not discuss it further.

The expression 'reflection' is certainly an inappropriate translation for 'glory'. A. Feuillet has demonstrated that the expression 'to be something's glory' usually indicates that the subject can therefore be proud of himself. As in **Pr 31:28-31** the woman

---

dale, David & Elouise Fraser, " A Biblical View of Women: Demythologizing Sexegisis," *Theology, News and Notes* (Pasadena, Fuller Theological Seminary Alumni, June 1975): pp. 14-18; Mary Evans, *Women in the Bible* (Exeter: The Paternoster Press, 1983): p. 86; Robins Scroggs, "Paul and Eschatological Woman," *Journal of the American Association for Religions (JAAR)* 40 (1972): pp. 283-303 and pp. 289-299, note 41; Katharine Bushnell, *101 Questions Answered: A Woman's Catechism – God's Word to Women,* (Southport, Great Britain: Lowes Ltd., n.d.): pp. 53-54. Assumes the meaning, 'support', but has apparently derived this from 'source'. Compare the discussion between the advocates of this view: J. A. Fitzmeyer, "Another Look at *kephale* in 1Corinthians 11.3," *New Testament Studies 35* (1989): pp. 503-522 and Wayne Grudem who has brought forward evidence to the contrary, "The Meaning of kephale ('Head'): A Response to Recent Studies," pp. 425-468 in John Piper, Wayne Grudem, ed. *Recovering Biblical Manhood and Womanhood* (Wheaton, Ill.: Crossway Books, 1991); Wayne Grudem, "Does kephale ('Head') Mean 'Source' or 'Authority over' in Greek Literature? A Survey of 2.336 Examples", *Trinity Journal 6* (1985): pp. 38-59, as well as Gordon Fee's criticism of Grudem in *The First Epistle to the Corinthians*, op. cit., pp. 502-503, note 42.

[221] See the discussion of the debate in David E. Blattenberger, *Rethinking 1Corinthians 11:2-16 through Archaeological and Moral-Rhetorical Analysis*, Studies in the Bible and Early Christianity, vol. 36, (Lewiston: Edwin Mellen Press, 1997), pp. 15-19, and the discussion between the advocates of this position: J. A. Fitzmeyer, "Another Look at kephale in 1Corinthians 11.3," *New Testament Studies 35* (1989), pp. 503-511, and: Wayne Grudem, "The Meaning of kephale ('Head'): A Response to Recent Studies," pp. 425-468 in: John Piper, Wayne Grudem (Ed.), *Recovering Biblical Manhood and Womanhood,* (Wheaton: Crossway Books, 1991); Wayne Grudem, "Does kephale ('Head') Mean 'Source' or 'Authority over' in Greek Literature? A Survey of 2,336 Examples," *Trinity Journal 6* (1985), pp. 38-59. Grudem brings several arguments against the interpretation. See also criticism of Grudem in : Gordon D. Fee, The First Epistle to the Corinthians, op. cit., pp. 502-503, Note 42.

[222] L. Ann Jervis, "But I Want to Know: Paul's Midrashic Intertextual Response to the Corinthian Worshipers (1Cor 11:2-16)," *Journal of Biblical Literature 112* (1993), pp. 231-246, pp. 240.

is the 'doxa' of her husband, his honor and pride.[223] Abel Isaksson has pointed out that one may arbitrarily assume another
meaning neither for 'glory' nor for 'image' (verse 7) than the cus-
tomary, positive one.[224]

The first word in verse 11, 'plen' is usually rendered *'never-*
theless', but actually means either 1) *'however' 'whereas'* which
introduces a contradictory argument, or 2) *'only' , at any rate'*
which concludes a statement by emphasizing its essential elements or by breaking it off and going on to a new subject, *'but*
rather'.[225]

Matthew and Luke use 'plen' to mean 'however' or 'whereas',
instead of *'alla'*. Paul however uses it in the sense of 'only' or 'at
any rate' which concludes the argument, emphasizing its essential
elements (See Eph 5:33; Php 1:18; 3:16; 4:14. For a non-Pauline
example, see Rev 2:25).[226]

Even exegetes who assume that Paul is in favor of a headcovering prefer the translation 'however' if verse 11 is begun with a
correction of the former statement:

"Plen introduces a correction of the traditional understanding
of Ge 2:18-22."[227]

One might wonder if the proponents of the quotation theory
had not drawn all their arguments from the arsenal of Bible criticism when they assume that the statements after verse 10 dis-

---

[223] A. Feuillet, "L'homme 'gloire de Dieu' et la femme 'gloire de l'homme' (I Cor., XI
7b)", *Revue Biblica 81* (1974): pp. 161-182; A. Feuillet, "La dignité et le role de la
femme d'après quelques texte pauliniens: comparaison avec l'Ancien Testament," *New
Testament Studies 21* (1975): pp. 157-191.

[224] Abel Isaksson, *Marriage and Ministry in the New Temple: A Study with Special
Reference to Mt. 19.3-12 and 1. Cor. 11.3-16* (Lund: Hakan Ohlsson, 1965): p. 173.

[225] Walter Bauer, Kurt and Barbara Aland, *Wörterbuch zum Neuen Testament*, op cit.,
col. 1345-1346 (including all NT occurrences of the word); A. Jaubert, "Le Voile des
Femmes (ICor. XI,2-16)", *New Testament Studies 18* (1972): pp. 419-430. Refers to
Friedrich Blass, Albert Debrunner, Friedrich Rehkopf, *Grammatik des neutesta-
mentlichen Griechisch* (Göttingen, Germany: 1979): pp.379-380 (§ 449.1+2). Compare
Norbert Baumert, *Antifeminismus bei Paulus?*, op. cit., p. 88.

[226] Blass, Albert Debrunner, Friedrich Rehkopf, *Grammatik des neutestamentlichen
Griechisch*, op. cit., pp. 379-380.

[227] Jerome Murphy-O'Connor, "Sex and Logic in 1Corinthians 11:2-16," op. cit., p.
497; similar David E. Blattenberger, *Rethinking 1Corinthians 11:2-16 ...*, op. cit., p. 20.

prove the view presented above. I certainly do not question Paul's authority, but I am interested in unraveling the true argumentation of the text. (Besides, this interpretation existed long before higher Bible criticism.) As a matter of fact, as far as the interpretation of this text is concerned, the Bible believing proponents of the scarf for women also share the opinion of proponents of higher criticism.

Let me note that many exegetes, both supporters of the alternative view and of the traditional view, consider 1Co 11:2 an ironic quotation of a Corinthian statement,[228] since Paul's arguments in verses 3-16 in any case contradict verse 2 which demonstrates that the Corinthians were not keeping Paul's orders. The same thing happens in Paul's comments on Communion in verses 17-34 in which he criticizes them for ignoring the truths he had taught them.[229]

Antoinette Clark Wire, in contradicting the quotation theory, has pointed out that Paul otherwise always clearly marks quotations in 1Co that such citations are always short, and that he always follows them immediately with a definite rebuttal (for example 1Co 1:12; 6:12-13; 7:1; 8:1-7; 15:12).[230] Thomas R. Schreiner has also objected to the quotation theory, because he considers the quotation too long, and because Paul does not clearly indicate that he is quoting.[231]

---

[228] E. Evans, *The Epistle of Paul the Apostle to the Corinthians* (Oxford: Clarendon Press, 1930) p. 117; James B. Hurley, "Did Paul Require Veils or Silence of Women? A Consideration of 1Cor. 11:2-16 and 1Cor. 14:33b-36," *Westminster Theological Journal 35* (1973): pp. 190-220; S. T. Lowrie, "I Corinthians XI and the Ordination of Women As Ruling Elders," *Princeton Theological Review 19* (1921) pp. 113-130, here p. 113, J. C. Hurd, *The Origin of ICorinthians* (New York: Seabury, 1965): pp. 182-184. On page 68 and page 90, note 2. Hurd offers many other more recent proponents of this view.

[229] Michael Molthagen, *Der Schleier im Christentum*, 10 pp, 2000, www.answering-islam.de/German/schleier/schleier_nt.pdf (used 1.3.2002) assumes that the second half of 1Co 11:3 belongs to the Corinthian position. It would be interesting to hear his reasons.

[230] Antoinette Clark Wire, *The Corinthian Woman Prophets* (Minneapolis: Fortress Press, 1990): pp. 229-230.

[231] Thomas R. Schreiner, "Head Coverings, Prophecies and the Trinity: 1Corinthians 11:2-16" in *Recovering Biblical Manhood and Womanhood,* op. cit., pp. 124-139.

Since the examples noted by Wire do not however so clearly indicate a citation as some exegetes would like to suggest, these texts also need to be individually examined. 1Co 8 also repeats and refutes longer chains of argument by the Corinthian church, not just single catchwords.

Daniel L. Segraves points out that no serious theologian ever taught the quotation theory – a popular argument of the establishment – and that it contradicts the nature of God's Word to cite someone other than God.[232] However, the Bible contains countless quotations – many are completely false and some from Satan himself. The reliablilty of Scripture means that such statements have been recorded accurately, not that God agrees with them.

Perhaps the statements are not direct citations, but the repetition of a view or even an ironic representation 'ad absurdum'.

Proposition 8

Most proponents of the alternative interpretation assume that Paul's quotation of the Corinthian position ends at verse 9.[233] **In this case, verse 10 reflects Paul's position. He thus gives the woman** *"authority over her head."* **The expression 'authority over' (***'exousia epi'***) always has this meaning in the New Testament and elsewhere** (for example, 'authority over demons'), is never used in a passive sense ('to have someone with authority over one'), and never refers to an object which lies on something else. 'To have authority over' means that the woman may decide for herself what she does with her head.

---

[232] Daniel L. Segraves, *Hair Length in the Bible: A Study of ICorinthians 11:2-16,* (Hazelwood: World Aflame Press, 1989), p. 58 (first edition1979 Women's Hair – The Long and Short of It).

[233] Thomas P. Shoemaker, "Unveiling of Equality: 1Corinthians 11:2-16," op. cit., pp. 61-62. See also Alan Padgett, "Paul on Women in the Church," op. cit., pp. 69-72. Padgett does not regard 'plen' at the beginning of verse 11 for the antithesis of verse 10 (Ibid., p. 72), but still containing the Corinthian position (Ibid., p. 39), but fails to resolve the contradiction.

The proposition in detail

1Co 11:10 is central to our perikope[234] and contains a comprehensive commandment, but is the most difficult verse in the whole text, for "the difficulties of v.10 surpass those of all other verses combined."[235] The central issue is which 'authority' is meant (Proposition 8) and why Paul refers to the angels (Proposition 9).

The two basic interpretation of 'authority' in 1Co 11:10, are according to Werner de Boor:

"The *'authority'* is either the husband's authority which the wife freely recognizes, or the woman's authority to pray and prophecy which she possesses only by submitting to the order of creation."[236]

'Authority (Gr. 'exousia') is never used in the New Testament to describe the man's position in relationship to the woman. When translations of the Bible render the term in verse 10 "an authority over her head" or "the sign of an authority over her head", they adapt the text to suit it to a particular interpretation. Robertson, for example, simply states that 'exousia' is an abbreviation for 'semeion exouias',[237] but like many other writers, offers no proof for the addition of the word 'sign'. Thomas R. Schreiner refers to Bauer's lexicon [238]for evidence that *'exousia'* means a symbol of submission; a case of circular reasoning, since not only Bauer, but other lexica, give only 1Co 11:10 as evidence.

---

[234] See Shoemakers graphic above under proposition 7 and the arguments in Sheila E. McGinn, "1Cor 11:10 and the Ecclesial Authority of Women," Listening (Romeville, IL, USA) 31 (1996) 2: pp. 91-104, p. 92.

[235] Jason David BeDuhn, "Because of the Angels: Unveiling Paul's Anthropology in 1Corinthians 11," *Journal of Biblical Literature 118* (1999), pp. 295-320, here p. 302.

[236] Werner de Boor, *Der Erste Brief des Paulus an die Korinther,* op. cit., p. 182.

[237] Archibald Thomas Robertson, *Word Pictures in the New Testament,* vol. 4, *The Epistles of Paul* (1931, repr. Grand Rapids, Mich.: Baker Book House, n.d.): p. 161.

[238] Thomas R. Schreiner, "Head Coverings, Prophecies and the Trinity: 1Corinthians 11:2-16," op. cit., p. 135; Walter Bauer, Kurt and Barbara Aland, *Wörterbuch zum Neuen Testament,* op. cit., col. 564, section 5.

Parallels are often drawn to references in which someone bears royal authority on his head (Gr. 'basileia'), meaning the crown as a symbol of royal authority,[239] but this parallel is no argument, since it refers to a different word,[240] and since the crown is a symbol of the wearer's own authority, not of someone else's authority over him.

Neither in the New Testament nor in the Septuaginta nor in the entire Greek literature can any example or parallel be found which would suggest that *'exousia'* might designate sign of submission or of authority.[241] Lexicons always cite 1Co 11:10 in an extra category.[242] Werner Foerster wonders, "... how the word came by this definition. It does not designate a 'sign of authority' or of anything else!"[243]

'Exousia' actually means 'the ability or permission to do something which is possible, the authorization or right to something, the power' or 'the means to exercise power.'

The distinguished historian, William Mitchell Ramsey, who defends the New Testament's credibility writes:

"... This seems so strange to the Western mind that the words have been generally reckoned among the most obscure in the whole of the Pauline writings. A vast amount has been written by commentators about them, almost entirely erroneous and

---

[239] Ibid., col 564, section 5, and Joseph H. Thayer, *Greek-English Lexicon of the New Testament*, op. cit., p. 225, section 1850 d; Thomas R. Schreiner, "Head Coverings, Prophecies and the Trinity," op. cit., p. 135 (uses Diodorus of Sicily 1.47.5, 60-30 BC as textual reference).

[240] William Mitchell Ramsay, *The Cities of St. Paul: Their Influence on His Life and Thought* (London: Hodder and Stoughton, 1908), p. 203 properly notes that Diodorus 1.47, in which the mother of the Egyptian king Osymandyas wears three crowns (*'basilea'*), or 'royal dignity', does not mean that she bears the symbol of another's royal authority on her head, but that she has won royal dignity in three ways; as daughter, mother and wife of the king.

[241] See the definitions in Werner Foerster, *"exestin, exousia ..."*, *Theologisches Wörterbuch zum Neuen Testament*, vol. 2, ed. Gerhard Kittel (Stuttgart, Germany: W. Kohlhammer, 1990): pp. 567-572.

[242] Ibid., p. 570-571; Walter Bauer, Kurt and Barbara Aland, *Wörterbuch zum Neuen Testament*, op. cit., col. 564, section 5; Joseph H. Thayer, *Greek-English Lexicon of the New Testament* (Grand Rapids, Mich.: Baker Book House, 1977): p. 225, section 1850 d.

[243] Werner Foerster, *"exestin, exousia ..."*, *Theologisches Wörterbuch zum Neuen Testament*, op. cit., p. 571.

misleading, and sometimes false to Greek language and its possibilities. Most of the ancient and modern commentators say that the 'authority' which the woman wears on her head is the authority to which she is subject – a preposterous idea which a Greek scholar would laugh at anywhere except in the New Testament, where (as they seem to think) Greek words may mean anything that commentators choose. Authority or power that belongs to the wearer, such power as the magistrate possesses in virtue of his office, was meant by the Greek word *exousia.*"[244]

Archibald Robertson and Alfred Plummer concur with Ramsay, without agreeing with his conclusion. Rather than attempting another translation or interpretation, they prefer to live with the dilemma.

"The difficulty is to see why the Apostle has expressed himself in this extraordinary manner. That 'authority' (exousia) is put for 'sign of authority'is not difficult; but why does St Paul say 'authority' when he means 'subjection'?"[245]

Leon Morris describes the dilemma in similar terms.

"The difficulty is that the context seems to demand a meaning like 'a symbol of subjection' (Mofatt) whereas the Greek word seems to mean 'a sign of her authority'. Indeed, Ramsay pours scorn on the idea that the term can indicate woman's subjection."[246]

---

[244] William Mitchell Ramsay, *The Cities of St. Paul*, op. cit., p. 203. On pages 202-205, he explains *'exousia'* in terms of the oriental use of the veil as a symbol of the woman's dignity and authority. At the same time, he represents the traditional view of 1Co 11:10, in that he considers the veil a sign of dignity, as does Ernst Lerle. See Leon Morris, *The First Epistle of Paul to the Corinthians* in *Tyndale New Testament Commentaries 7* (1958, repr., Grand Rapids, Mich.,: Wm B. Eerdmans, 1979): pp. 153-154.

[245] Archibald Robertson, Alfred Plummer, *A Critical and Exegetical Commentary on the First Epistle of St Paul to the Corinthians* in *The International Critical Commentary* (1914, repr. Edinburgh: T. & T. Clark, 1950): pp. 232-233.

[246] Leon Morris, *The First Epistle of Paul to the Corinthians*, op. cit., pp. 153-154. "Mofatt" refers to the interpretation in: James Moffat, *The First Epistle of Paul to the Corinthians* in *The Mofatt New Testament Commentary* (London: Hodder & Stoughton, 1943).

The dilemma exists, however, only as long as one assumes that the context demands a particular interpretation. If we disregard that interpretation, there is nothing to contradict the clear meaning of the Greek term: The woman has authority over her head. For this reason, advocates of the traditional translation still point out that 'authority' can only be understood as the the woman's active authority over her own head.[247]

Gordon D. Fee mentions the same dilemma, but chooses for that reason the meaning of the Greek text rather than the traditional interpretation.

> "The problem with this view is, that there is no documentation that *exousia* had ever taken on a passive meaning or that the idiom, 'to have authority over' had ever referred to anyone other than the subject of the sentence."[248]

Gerhard Kittel conjectures that Paul is making an Aramaic play on words, since Aramaic has two similar sounding words for 'authority' and for 'veil' – a complete covering, not a scarf; but this explanation, as do other similar attempts,[249] ignores the fact that the Corinthians spoke Greek and could not have known which play on words would be meant if the expression were translated into Aramaic.[250] The word 'authority' can only be identified with a 'covering', if one assumes that Paul is associating the term with

---

[247] See, for example: Jason David BeDuhn, "Because of the Angels: Unveiling Paul's Anthropology in 1Corinthians 11," *Journal of Biblical Literature 118* (1999), pp 295-320, pp. 302-303; Sheila E. McGinn, "1 Cor11:10 and the Ecclesiastical Authority of Women," *Listening* (Romeville, IL, USA) 31 (1996) 2: pp. 91-104, pp. 96-98.

[248] Gordon D. Fee, *The First Epistle to the Corinthians*, op. cit., p. 519.

[249] See G. Schwarz, "Exousian echein epi tes kephales? (1. Korinther 11:10)," *Zeitschrift für neutestamentliche Wissenschaft 70* (1979): p. 249 who refutes Kittel's explanation, but offers a quite similar one based on an Aramaic word which can mean either 'power' or 'headcovering'.

[250] For further attempts using plays on words and other languages, see; Max Küchler, *Schweigen, Schmuck und Schleier, Novum Testamentum et orbis antiquus 1* (Freiburg, Switzerland: Universitätsverlag and Göttingen, Germany: Vandenhoeck & Ruprecht, 1986): pp. 89-92 (Compare the list of theories as to the meaning of the veil on pages 92-98).

a meaning otherwise unknown in Greek or in the New Testament.[251]

> In reference to the term 'authority over', Mary Evans writes: "Some have taken the 'authority' (exousia), as the authority of the husband over the wife, but this is extremely unlikely as there is no parallel for exousia being used in the passive sense that would be necessary if this interpretation were correct, and there is nothing in the context to indicate that the word was being used in anything other than the normal way."[252]

Even if 'exousia' by itself could designate a symbol of submission under a power, and if 'to have authority' were passive, the addition of the preposition 'epi' disrupts the whole argument. The expression 'exousia epi' ('authority over') is used frequently in Scripture, where it always means the active authority over a person or thing. The same expression is used for example to describe the power of Christ and of the Angel of Judgment in Mt 9:6, Mk 2; Lk 5:34, Re 11:6 and 4:13.[253] Archibald Robertson and Alfred Plummer give the following examples: Re 11:6; 14:13 and 20:6, as well as parallels such as Ro 9:21; 1 Co 7:37; and Da 3:20 (LXX).[254] Gordon D. Fee suggests the examples Lk 19:11; Re 11:6,14,18; 16:9; 20:6 (all include 'to have') and Lk 9:1; 10:19; Re 2:26; 6:8; 13:7 (without 'to have').[255] Fee's translation of 1Co 11:10 follows John Lightfoot's position of 1675: "For this reason the woman ought to have freedom over her head to do as she wishes."[256] S. T. Lowrie also emphasizes that 'exousia' could

---

[251] M. D. Hooker, "Authority on Her Head: An Examination of ICorinthians xi.10," *New Testament Studies 10* (1964): pp. 410-416.

[252] Mary Evans, *Women in the Bible*, op. cit., pp. 90-91.

[253] Richard and Catherine Clark Kroeger, "Sexual Identity in Corinth," *The Reformed Journal 28* vol. 12 (Dec. 1978): pp. 11-15.

[254] Archibald Robertson, Alfred Plummer, A Critical and Exegetical Commentary on the First Epistle of St Paul to the Corinthians, op. cit., p. 232.

[255] Gordon D. Fee, The First Epistle to the Corinthians, op. cit., p. 520, note. 29.

[256] Ibid. p. 520 from John Lightfoot whole Writings ... Volume XII., op. cit., p. 517-519. Fee also refers to Philipp Payne, *Man and Woman: One in Christ* (Baker Book House: Grand Rapids, 1987): p. 50-51 and Alan Padgett. "Paul on Women in the Church," op. cit., p. 78.

never designate a symbol of submission to an authority, and translated, „ ... *the woman ought to have power over her head"* or *„ The woman ought to have a right over her head. "*[257]

M. D. Hooker shares this opinion, and considers the usage of 'exousia' in 1Co 7:37 an example for the sense of 'liberty', but believes that the woman exercises this liberty by veiling herself,[258] fails however to explain why veiling should be a sign of feminine authority and to what extent a woman then obtains liberty over her head. Others suggests similar interpretations, that the 'exousia' of a woman in veiling her head gives her the authority to prophecy.[259] But I repeat my objects against the identification of 'exousia' with a garment.

Richard and Catherine Clark Kroeger go a step further and interpret the 'authority over her head' to mean the woman's authority over men, since Paul has just called the man the head of the woman. (vs. 3).[260] They point out that Paul has already discussed the man's 'exousia' over the woman, as well as the 'exousia' of the woman over the man (using the appropriate verb. *"The woman has no authority over her own body; her husband does; in the same way, the husband has no authority over his own body; his wife does."* (1Co 7:4). Even though this view of our text makes no sense, in my opinion, and since the 'head' here probably means a part of the body rather than husband, the parallel shows how varied and multi-leveled biblical terminology can be, and how little presuppositions about terminology concerning

---

[257] S. T. Lowrie, "ICorinthians XI and the Ordination of Women As Ruling Elders," *Princeton Theological Review 19* (1921): pp. 113-130, here pp. 123-124.

[258] M. D. Hooker, "Authority on Her Head: An Examination of ICor. xi. 10," op. cit, p. 413.

[259] For example Ibid., p. 415-416; D. Ellul, "?'Sois belle et tais-toi!' Est-ce vraiment ce que Paul a dit?: A propos de ICo 11,2-16," *Foi et Vie* (Paris) 88 (1989) 5: pp. 49-58; A. Pérez Gordo, "¿Es el velo en 1Co 11,2-16 símbolo de libertad o de submisión?," *Burgense* (Burgo) 29 (1988): pp. 337-366; A. Feuillet, "Le signe de puissance sur la tete de la femme, 1Co 11,10," *Nouvelle Revue Théologique 95* (1973): pp. 945-954; Elizabeth Schüssler Fiorenza, *In Memory of Her* (New York, 1983): pp. 226-230, here p. 228; C. K. Barrett, *A Commentary on The First Epistle to the Corinthians* (London: A & A Black, 1971²): p. 255.

[260] Richard and Catherine Clark Kroeger, "Sexual Identity in Corinth," op. cit.

the relationship between man and woman do justice to the biblical material.

The identification of the 'authority' with a headcovering is only possible when we identify 'authority' with a 'symbol of her authority' and define the covering as the proof of her authority, as F. F. Bruce, Ernst Lerle[261] and Abel Isaksson (with a particular exaggeration of the covering as the authority to prophecy[262]) have done.

It would be more sensible to explain that Paul is giving the woman authority over herself[263] and over her head. Alan Padgett well, summarizes this position which has been held for several centuries:

"From this discussion, it can be concluded that the phrase in v. 10 means: women ought to have freedom, right or power to do what they wish with their heads. In the context of this passage, it would mean that women ought to have the right to chose whatever hairstyle they wish."[264]

Of cause this would not include hairstyle alone, but also whether or not and how a woman wants to cover her head.

This meaning for 'exousia' has remained constant up until now.[265] Even in modern Greek, we can find no examples in which 'exousia' is used passively or symbolically.

Proposition 9

Some proponents of the alternative interpretation add verse 10 to the Corinthian position because of its apparently unexplainable reference to the angels. The angels are thus not 'lustful angels', but the Jewish or Gnostic heresies which Paul frequently had to

---

[261] F. F. Bruce, 1 and 2Corinthians, *op. cit.,* p. 106.

[262] Abel Isaksson, Marriage and Ministry in the New Temple, op.cit., pp. 178-179.

[263] Cynthia L. Thompson, "Hairstyles, Head-coverings and St. Paul: Portraits from Roman Corinth," *Biblical Archaeologist 51* (1988): pp. 99-115; David & Elouise Fraser, "A Biblical View of Women," op. cit., p.17; James B. Hurley, "Did Paul Require Veils or Silence of Women?," op. cit., pp. 207-208.

[264] Alan Padgett, "Paul on Women in the Church," op. cit, p. 72. See also, for example, John Lightfoot whole Writings ... Volume XII., op. cit, pp. 517-519.

[265] G. Giannakomoulou, *Ariston Ellenogermanikon Lexikon*, Tl. A, (Michigan Press: (MI); P. Koutsoumpos: Athen, 1972): p. 435.

oppose in Corinth. For this reason, there is still no satisfactory explanation for the reference to angels. *The possibility that Paul mentions them only because the Corinthians were worshipping them, harmonizes with the interpretation that verse 10 includes Paul's reply. Paul would then be reminding his readers of his statement in 1Co 6:3 that Christians, both men and women, will judge the angels. Therefore, women are certainly able to decide about their own heads.*

The proposition in detail

1Co 11:10, with its reference to angels, is the most difficult verse in the New Testament. I. Broer writes,

"No satisfactory explanation for the difficult verse, 1Co 11:10, and for its use of *exousia* has been found."[266]

It is not necessary to go through all of the various explanations of the words, "because of the angels," suggested by the proponents of other interpretations.[267] Are these 'lustful angels' whose passions can be restrained by headcoverings? Are they protective angels, since the text literally says, "because of the angels"?[268] Is Paul speaking of angels who attend the service, as some have concluded from parallels with Qumran documents?[269] Are the angels simply symbols of God's presence?[270] Are the angels the church leaders, as they may be in Revelations 2-3? Does Paul mention the angels, because they themselves cover their faces in

[266] I. Broer, "exousia," Col. 23-29 in: Horst Balz, Gerhard Schneider, ed. *Exegetisches Wörterbuch zum Neuen Testament*, vol. 2, (Stuttgart: W. Kohlhammer, 1981): col. 29; compare the quotations in Paul Petry, "Das verschleierte Haupt," *Licht und Leben 67* (1956): pp. 52-54.

[267] See the examples in Max Küchler, Schweigen, Schmuck und Schleier, *Novum Testamentum et orbis antiquus 1*, (Freiburg: Universitätsverlag and Göttingen: Vandenhoeck & Ruprecht, 1986) pp. 98-102.

[268] Katharine Bushnell, *101 Questions Answered*, op.cit., pp. 43-45.

[269] J. A. Fitzmeyer, "A Feature of Qumran Angelology and The Angels of ICor xi. 10," *New Testament Studies 4* (1957): pp. 48-58.

[270] Heinrich Schlier, "kephale, anakephalaioomai," in: Gerhard Kittel, ed., *Theologisches Wörterbuch zum Neuen Testament*, vol. 3. (repr., Stuttgart: W. Kohlhammer, 1990): p. 678-679.

God's presence (Isa 6:2)[271] – which however describes a complete veiling, and fails to explain why the man needs no such covering.

I find most of these explanations too speculative. *Some may clarify the reference to the angels, but none explain why only the woman requires a covering, and not the man as well.* The reference to the angels is the major reason that most proponents of the quotation theory include verse 10 in the Corinthian position. If the reference were not there, we could agree with the view that Paul begins his refutation in verse 10. As it is, however, the quotation theory offers no reasonable explanation for the use of angels to justify any sort of commandments, specifically the commandment to cover oneself. After all, the angels serve the believers as God's messengers (Heb 1:14) and will be judged by them one day (1Co 6:3).

In my opinion only two proponents of the quotation theory have convincing reasons for including verse 10 in Paul's argumentation. Alan Padgett assumes that the word 'angels' (Gr. *'angelos'* 'Messenger') refers to feminine 'messengers,' such as Pricilla, Phoebe or others of Paul's assistants who could not be expected to obey Corinthian rules unknown to other churches.[272] Padgett himself admits that this is only a suggestion not any better grounded than others that have been made.[273]

Philip Payne interprets the reference to the angels in relationship to 1Co 6:3 that the Christians will judge the angels: Since women will one day judge angels, they now have the authority to decide about their own bodies.[274]

This idea could lead further, even though it lacks sufficient documentation. Paul's own view, stated in this very letter, that

---

[271] Archibald Thomas Robertson, *Word Pictures in the New Testament*, vol. IV, op.cit., p. 161.

[272] Alan Padgett, *Paul on Women in the Church*, op. cit., p. 81-82.

[273] Ibid., p. 82.

[274] Philipp Payne, *Man and Woman: One in Christ*, (Grand Rapids: Baker Book House, 1987): p. 51-53; see also: Gordon D. Fee, *The First Epistle to the Corinthians*, op. cit., p. 522.

the angels will be subject to the believers' judgment,[275] can also be found in contemporary Jewish literature.[276] Perhaps Paul is guarding against exaggerated respect for angels which could lead to idolatry, such as was the case in Gnostic groups. The Epistle to the Colossians refers directly to such a misdirected reference to angels:

> *"Let no man beguile you of your reward in a voluntary humility and worshipping of angels, intruding into those things which he hath not seen, vainly puffed up by his fleshly mind."* (Col 2:18)

If we assume that Paul is opposing the threat of angel worship, then 1Co 11:10 would justify the woman's authority over her head with the reminder that Christians are above the angels. He begins his argument in verse 10a, attacks angel worship with bitter irony in 10b, referring to the position of the angels in contrast to that of the woman; since women will one day judge the angels, they now are justified in deciding for themselves.

Proposition 10

The Old Testament confirms the interpretation that Paul is not commanding women to wear long hair and a veil and men to wear their hair short, for it describes many men with long hair (the priests and the Nazi-rites) and women who prayed without a headcovering. The veil was not a symbol of dignity, but could also have negative connotations; Tamar covered her head in order to disguise herself as a prostitute (Ge 38:14-15).

The proposition in detail

The veil could, however, also have positive connotations, in the wedding night, for example. Jack Deere, commenting on SS 4:1, writes

---

[275] See also: Lukas Vischer, *Die Auslegungsgeschichte von 1Kor 6,1-11: Rechtsverzicht und Schlichtung, Beiträge zur Geschichte der neutestamentlichen Exegese* (Tübingen, Germany: J. C. B. Mohr, 1955) p. 10-11.

[276] Ibid., pp. 10-12.

that women in the Ancient Near East usually wore a veil only at their own wedding. They removed it when they entered the bridal chamber (which is why Rebecca veiled her face, when Isaac, her future husband approached. Ge 24:65). Laban took advantage of the custom to deceive Jacob by marrying him to Lea instead to Rachel (Ge 29:19-25).[277]

The Old Testament clearly refutes the idea that Paul expects men to serve God uncovered and with short hair, while women are to approach the Lord veiled with long hair. Can *"Nature"* contradict God's Old Testament directions? (1 Kor 11:14)

I find *three reasons* against the derivation of commandments on hair styles and veils from the Old Testament:

1. The Old Testament contexts are historical narratives and lack any indication of God's opinion on the subject.
2. The directions about hair styles are given to very different groups (priests or Nazirites).
3. The various garments and hairstyles described would be completely contradictory, if they were all obligatory.

Short hair, by the way, was in no way typical for Old Testament men. On the contrary, men often wore their hair long and flowing (2Sa 14:26; Eze 8:3).[278] Since shaving the head was part of mourning rites,[279] short hair must have been an exception to the rule.

"As far as hair styles are concerned, the Hebrews shared the opinion that long hair and a long beard were part of the man's ornamentation and dignity. ... The law forbids shaving the head ..."[280]

---

[277] Jack S. Deere, "Das Hohelied," pp. 697-720 in: John F. Walvoord, Roy F. Zuck, *Das Alte Testament erklärt und ausgelegt*, vol. 2, (Neuhausen, Germany: Hänssler, 1991).

[278] Bernhard Kötting, "Haar," Col. 177-203 in: Theodor Klausner e. a., ed., *Reallexikon für Antike und Christentum*, vol. 13 (Stuttgart: Anton Hiersemann, 1986): col. 188.

[279] Gustav Stählin, "kapetos, kopto ...," pp. 829-860 in: Gerhard Kittel, ed., *Theologisches Wörterbuch zum Neuen Testament*, vol. 3, (repr. Stuttgart, Germany: W. Kohlhammer, 1990): here p. 836 cites: Isa 22,12; Jer 16,6; Eze 24,16-17,22-23 (as well as the LXX and later Jewish writings).

[280] Benzinger, "Haar," pp. 276-278 in: Albert Hauck, ed., *Realencyklopädie für protestantische Theologie und Kirche*, vol. 7, (Leipzig: J. C. Hinrichs, 1899³): here p. 277;

At the same time, men frequently covered their heads, particularly the prophets, such as Moses (Ex 19:13), David (2Sa 15:30-32), Elijah (1Ki 19:13) or Ezekiel (Eze 24:15-21). A headcovering was prescribed for the priests during their service in the Sanctuary, as we see in the laws given for the priests in Lev 8:9,13; 10:6; 21:10. Abel Isaksson suggests that God is wearing a priestly headcovering in Da 7:9.[281]

2Co 3:18 is often cited in this context:

"But we all, with open face beholding as in a glass the glory of the Lord, are changed into the same image from glory to glory, even as by the Spirit of the Lord."

If we assume that this verse describes an essential difference between the Old Testament and the New that the Old Testament veil has been put away, we must then ask why this new liberty should not apply to women.

The *Nazirite vow* (Nu 6:1-21) was a special case which demanded abstinence from alcohol and shaving the head. In reply to the argument that this only involved a limited amount of time, so that the hair would not have grown very long, let me point out that some men took the vow for their whole lives; Samuel (1Sa 1:11) and Samson (Jdg 13:5) are the best examples. Samson's hair was cut only once, by his lover, Delilah which caused the Lord to abandon him (Jdg 16:15-22). John the Baptist was probably also a Nazirite (Lk 1:15; Mt 3:4). John Lightfoot considers Absolom to have been a Nazirite as well (2Sa 15:7-8)[282]

Note that Paul was under a Nazirite vow during his stay in Corinth, and thus had long hair at the time.[283] Not until he had left Corinth for the suburb Cenchrea did he cut his hair (Ac 18:18).

includes further OT Examples (mockery of baldness, whereas baldness was 'pure' according to Lev 13:40-41). The reference to Dt 14:1; Lev 19,27 is, however, according to Benzinger, relative, since only parts of the head may be shaved. Compare the ban on trimming the corners of the beard and the ban on shaving parts of the priest's head. Carl Friedrich Keil, *Leviticus, Numeri und Deuteronomium*, (repr. from 1870², Giessen, Germany: Brunnen Verlag, 1987³): p. 141.

[281] Abel Isaksson, Marriage and Ministry in the New Temple, op. cit., p. 174.

[282] John Lightfoot whole Writings ... Volume XII., op. cit., p. 516.

[283] Ralph Woodrow, *Women's Adornment: What does the Bible Really Say* (Riverside, USA: Ralph Woodrow Evangelistic Association, 1976): pp. 47-48.

His arrest in Jerusalem also had to do with a Nazirite vow, for when he underwent the ritual purification with four other Nazirites, and paid for their haircuts as well as for his own, the Jews assumed that he had done it for non-Jews (Ac 21:23-34).[284]

Ac 18:18 uses the same word for 'to shave' and 'to have shaved' ('keiro'), that Paul uses in 1Co 11:6,[285] and Ac 21:24 uses same word for 'to shave' as 1Co 11:5-6.[286]

The Old Testament only mentions a few short-haired men. Eze 44:20 commands the priests of the new temple to wear short hair.[287] But who are these priests? Why are they commanded to dress differently from the Aaronic priests? Note that Eze 44:18 commands them to wear the priestly headcovering. Whoever uses 1Co 11:2-16 to insist that men wear short hair, must find an explanation for this paradox.

The Old Testament is silent about women's hair. Most women wore their hair long, but this is never commanded. Besides, women's hair was usually worn open and uncovered, for "long, flowing hair was considered the woman's ornament."[288] (See SS 4:1). Women must have often appeared uncovered, for the Bible often comments on the beauty of their faces. (Rebecca Ge 26:7; Rachel Ge 29:10-11). Eli could see Hannah's lips moving while she prayed (1Sa 1:12-13). *Judah even considered Thamar a prostitute, because she had covered herself with a veil (Ge 38:14-15).*

---

[284] The Jews had seen "Trophimus, the Epheser" (Ac 21,29) and thought that Paul had financed his Nazirite vows. If we wanted to exaggerate, we could wonder if Trophimus didn't have such long hair that he could have been confused with a Nazirite.

[285] Walter Bauer, Kurt and Barbara Aland, W*örterbuch zum Neuen Testament* (Berlin, Germany: Walter de Gruyter, 1988[6]): col. 868; Joseph H. Thayer, *Greek-English Lexicon of the New Testament*, op. cit., p. 343 (Nr. 2751).

[286] Compare Walter Bauer, Kurt and Barbara Aland, *Wörterbuch zum Neuen Testament* (Berlin, Germany: Walter de Gruyter, 1988[6]): col. 868; Joseph H. Thayer, *Greek-English Lexicon of the New Testament*, op. cit., p. 343 (no. 2751).

[287] Hans-Josef Klauck, *Erster Korintherbrief, Die Neue Echter Bibel 7* (Würzburg: Echter Verlag, 1984): p. 78.

[288] Benzinger, "Haar," op. cit., p. 277.

Even if we could prove that Old Testament women were veiled, we must answer John Lightfoot's question:

"Where, I ask, is a veil demanded as a sign of such submission?"[289]

Proposition 11

Propositions 1-6 and 9-10 are still valid, even if the so-called 'quotation theory' of Propositions 7-8 is rejected. Even if a person disagrees with Propositions 7-8, he should still take the others into consideration, for they are still valid, even if the entire text represents Paul's opinion.

In that case, Paul is describing the particular role of the man, then reminds the Corinthians that men cannot exist without women, and then contradicts the requirement of headcovering for women with a reference to Nature and to the woman's natural headcovering, her hair.

Proposition 12

We can still be consider the text valid for our modern day and age, without being confused by the reference to a custom which is not specifically defined. Paul who generally rejects the equation of rules not required by the Word of God with God's Law, agrees with Jesus' words against the Pharisees in Mk 7:1-23. Since neither the Old Testament nor any other text in the New ever require any veiling of women, either in general or in worship, 1Co 11:1-16 is too disputed to permit any comprehensive conclusions about dress codes for women.

Proposition 13

If the alternative interpretation of 1Co 11:1-16 is correct, that does not mean that Paul is repealing the biblical distinction between man's duties and women's. He himself clearly distinguishes between the two and defends the difference in other texts. The problem is that the Corinthians had drawn wrong conclusions from correct statements.

---

[289] On Eze 44 und 1 Co 11,2-16 see: Abel Isaksson, *Marriage and Ministry in the New Temple*, op. cit.

This is typical of his problems with the Corinthians, as two examples demonstrate. In 1Co 5:9-13, some church members had concluded from Paul's instructions about church discipline, that they should also avoid unbelievers, an idea Paul refutes in 1Co 5:10,12,13). In chapters 8-10, he corrects the misunderstanding of some believers who considered the fact that there is only one God, and that other gods are nothing (8:4-7) a justification for participation in idol worship (8:7-11) which he energetically rejects (10:14-22).

The following chapter deals with Paul's dispute with his Corinthian opponents in order to substantiate the 13th Proposition.

4. Quotations and Irony in 1Corinthians

A typical characteristic of 1Co is Paul's way of dealing with his opponents' arguments by first quoting their position and by then using their words in his own argumentation. In no other epistle does he reply so directly to the reports, questions and letters of a local church, as he does in the epistles to the Corinthians. A short review of the letters' history and the relationship of the Corinthian church to Paul will clarify the background for this situation.

4.1. The Emergence of the Corinthian Church

The History of the Corinthian Church and the Letters to the Corinthians (51-55 AD)

A. *The Church is founded (Ac 18:1-17)*
Paul came to Corinth from Athens alone (Ac 18:1-17) in *'all weakness'* (1Co 2:1-5). He works in his profession as tentmaker in Aquila' workshop (Ac 18:2-3). After being thrown out of the synagogue, he continues his preaching in the house next-door (vs 7) which leads to the conversion of the synagogue's chairman, Crispus (vs 8). In the mean time, Timothy and Silas return, bringing an encouraging report from the church in Thessalonika (1Th 3-17).Some time later, Paul and his colleagues move with Aquila and Priscilla to Kenchrea (Ac 18:18), Phoebe's church (Ro 16:1-2), and then to Ephesus (Ac 18:18-22). In Ephesus, the Jewish speaker Apollos is converted and receives intensive instruction from Priscilla and Aquila (Ac 18:24-28); Paul is apparently on another journey (Ac 19:1). Apollos, with the approval of Paul and his assistants, moves to Ephesus (Ac 18:27-28), where he disputes publicly with the Jews (Ac 18:28) and *'waters'* the church with further doctrine (1Co 3:6; 1:12; 4:6). Some parties in the church identify themselves with Paul, Apollos or even with Christ – without their consent, some refer to Peter (1Co 1:12). Whether Peter or Christians from Jerusalem had ever come to Corinth we do not know (2Co 11:5), nor do we know whether the reference to Peter concerned any specific issue. At any rate, the different parties refered to their chosen 'head' without ever having consulted them!

B. Paul's first letter (no longer available)

In his first letter which has been lost (1Co 5:9), Paul deals primarily with sexual immorality (1Co 5:9,11) which the church completely misunderstands (1Co 5:10-13).

C. Members of Cloe's household tell Paul of the situation in Corinth

Members of Cloe's household visit Paul (1Co 1:11) and tell him about the dissention in the church (1Co 1:11-12).

D. An embassy from the church visits Paul

Stephan, Fortunatus and Achaicus visit Paul as representatives of the Corinthian church and encourage him (1Co 16:17-18). They bring him a written list of the church's questions which he answers in the First Epistle to the Corinthians.

E. Paul's second letter; our 1Corinthians

Paul writes a letter in which he refers to the report brought by Chloe's friends (1Co 1.6; particularly 1:11 and 5:1), and deals with the Corinthians' written questions (1Co 7-6; particularly 7:1; 7:25; 8:1; 9:3; 10:1; 11:2-3; 11:17; 12:1; 14;26; 15:1; 16:1). The major issues which he addresses are the divisive parties in the church. He stands between the fronts of those who deny his authority and those who use his name, as well as between libertines and ascetics. His concrete expectations consist above all in the demand of church discipline in a specific case.

F. Paul sends Timothy to Corinth and announces his own visit

Paul sends Timothy to Corinth, perhaps with 1Co (16:10-11). The information in Ac 19:22, however, make it seem unlikely that Timothy arrived in Corinth.

G. Paul visits the church. 'The sorrowful visit'

Paul visits the church, but is unsuccessful which grieves both sides (2Co 2:1-4; 12:14; 13:1-2).

H. Paul's third letter: the 'sorrowful letter' (now lost)

Paul writes a letter as sorrowful as his letter had been, and has it delivered by Titus (2Co 2:4; 7:8-9).

I. Titus returns to Paul and reports of the changed situation in Corinth

After delivering the letter and addressing the matters at hand, Titus returns to Paul to inform him about the changes (2Co 7:5-16). Restless, Paul had been traveling, and only finds Titus after a long search in Macedonia (2Co 2:13). The Corinthians repent.

J. Paul's fourth letter: our 2Corinthians

Paul reacts to the news with a fourth letter, in which he instructs the church to forgive those who had repented after being excommunicated, and to take them back into the fellowship (2Co 2:5-11). He courts their love, and requests money for the church in Jerusalem, defends himself against various accusations with reference to his pure motives (5:11-6:10), his weakness which stands in bitter contrast to the strength claimed by the self-proclaimed apostles who confuse the church (10:1-12,18). He finally announces a final visit (13:1-10).

K. Paul visits Corinth

He seems to have carried out this final visit and collected their contribution for Jerusalem (13:1-10).

L. Later mention

According to a letter by the Roman presbyter, Clement of Rome (95 AD) to the church in Corinth, Paul was still accorded great respect.

4.2 Paul in Cross-fire[290]

C. S. Lewis writes appropriately:

> "The devil ... always sends errors into the world in pairs – pairs of opposites. And he always encourages us to spend a lot of time thinking which is the worse. You see why, of course? He relies on your extra dislike of the one error to draw you gradually into the opposite one. But do not let us be fooled. We have to keep our eyes on the goal and go straight through between both errors." [291]

---

[290] Any earlier version was printed as, "Paulus zwischen Irrtum und Irrtum". *Bibel und Gemeinde 90* (1990): pp. 249-263.

[291] C. S. Lewis, *Mere Christianity*, (New York: The Macmillan Company), 1952, p. 160.

The Corinthian church was divided on almost all issues.[292] Paul almost never conceded completely to one party or the other, but admonished both, for neither reflected God's divine thought. Let us examine some of the issues:

Example: For and Against Paul (1Co 1-4)

Some of the Corinthians honored Paul so highly that he was forced to ask, *"was Paul crucified for you?"* – Towards others who rejected his authority completely, he insisted on his apostolic calling. Both parties endangered the truth that Paul, as an apostle called by God, had received great truths, but was still only one of God's servants; one group by making him the center of attention, the other – perhaps as a reaction against the first – by scorning him, as well as the revelation which he brought them.

Paul replied that the important issue was not his person, but the divine commission and the divine revelation of Scripture. Anyone who deserts biblical teaching is arrogant.

"And these things, brethren, I have in a figure transferred to myself and to Apollos for your sakes; that ye might learn in us not to think of men above that which is written, that no one of you be puffed up for one against another." (1Co 4:6).

The rejection of an unbiblical opinion is, however, no guarantee against error and arrogance! In Paul's opinion, the problem lay in the fact that the Corinthians appealed to all sorts of revelations and dogmas which went beyond the binding decrees of Scripture. Instead of referring to what God had already clearly revealed, they appealed to some apostle, some teacher or even Christ Himself, playing each off against the other, although all of these teachers taught the same truths through varying gifts and commissions.

Example: Church Discipline (1Co 5-6)

One of the major issues in 1Co was the lack of church discipline. The church tolerated people whose conduct showed clearly that they had turned their backs on God. Real love would have set

---

[292] Karl Wieseler, *Zur Geschichte der neutestamentlichen Schriften und des Christentums*, (J. C. Hinrich'sche Buchhandlung: Leipzig), 1880, p. 1-53.

them before the consequence, excommunication, in order to provide them with a last chance to repent. When the church later complies with Paul's instructions, the excommunication actually succeeds (2Co).

Interestingly enough, the same Paul who demanded discipline, also insisted that repentance be answered with renewal of fellowship (2Co 2:5-11) which some over-eager members, formerly opposed to discipline, now wanted to refuse.

Clearly, another current of opinion existed which believed in discipline, but overextended Paul's insistence on refusing contact to immoral or idolatrous church members to unbelievers. The apostle failed to see any positive zeal in this idea, but criticized the overzealous just as much as the over-lenient members.

"I wrote unto you in an epistle not to company with fornicators: Yet not altogether with the fornicators of this world, or with the covetous, or extortioners, or with idolaters; for then must ye needs go out of the world. But now I have written unto you not to keep company, if any man that is called a brother be a fornicator, or covetous, or an idolater, or a railer, or a drunkard, or an extortioner; with such an one no not to eat. For what have I to do to judge them also that are without? Do not ye judge them that are within? But them that are without God judgeth. Therefore put away from among yourselves that wicked person." (5:9-13)

The same Corinthian believers who had tolerated adultery in their own midst, now required all Christians to avoid contact with non-Christian adulterers instead of bringing them the good news of God's grace and forgiveness.

Example: Marital Love (1Co 6-7)

The issue of sexuality also had to be defended on both sides. One party considered visits to bordellos harmless, while the other considered even sex within marriage unspiritual. Paul points out on the one hand that our bodies are the temple of the Holy Spirit (6:19). On the other hand, he reminds the church of of marital duty in sexual matters; a 'platonic' marriage is dangerous (7:5).

He is not willing to ally himself with either group, for the only way to defeat error is with divinely revealed truth.

The issue of sexuality is an example of the way that both unbiblical extremes have determined church history up until modern times. Periods of libertine immorality alternate with periods of extreme prudery, each movement citing the section of Paul's epistle which suits them best. Biblical doctrine criticizes both extremes, for God created sex for joy in marriage, but forbids every other sort of sexuality.

Example: Meat Offered to Idols (1Co 8-10)

The most detailed example of the problems in Corinth is the question of meat offered to idols. The eighth and tenth chapters of the letter are often misunderstood, because interpreters ignored the fact that Paul is answering two contrary opinions.

One Side: Paul on idolatry (1Co 8-10:22)

On the one hand, some Corinthian believers saw nothing wrong in participating in pagan sacrifices, justifiying themselves by claiming a special 'knowledge' which Paul, however, speaks of with bitter irony (8:1-3).

"For if any man see thee which hast knowledge sit at meat in the idol's temple, shall not the conscience of him which is weak be emboldened to eat those things which are offered to idols." (1Co 8:10)

These believers justified their behavior with the truth that there are no other gods besides God. Paul first attempts to show them that the danger of their example to weaker Christians should be enough to keep them from idolatrous practices. In chapter 9, he offers several examples of situations in which he had done without in order to help others.

Gordon D. Fee suggests that 8:1-10:22 concerns participation in pagan cult meals which Paul had already forbidden in an earlier letter. His statements in chapter 8 deal with his opponents' arguments, while Paul enlarges on his prohibition in chapter 10. The apologia in chapter 9 is perhaps a reply to a Corinthian rejection of Paul's authority to forbid visits to the temples by pointing out that he also adapted to his surrounding (9:19-22).

If we do not emphasize the relationship between chapters 9 and 10 with chapter 8, we ignore Paul's actual reply in chapter 8 to the question whether participation in idolatrous practices is allowed. It is important to recognize that chapter 8 is only a preliminary statement which is clarified in detail in chapter 10; otherwise chapter 10 is left up in the air.

In chapter 10, Paul first reminds the Corinthians of the negative example of the Israelites who added idolatry to immorality and complaining:

"Neither be ye idolaters, as were some of them; as it is written: The people sat down to eat and drink, and rose up to play." *(1Co 10:7)*

That Paul is criticizing the *'knowledge'* of the believers who participated in idolatrous sacrifices becomes clear in verse 14.

"Therefore, my dearly beloved, flee from idolatry" (1Co 10:14).

After explaining that idolatry is inconsistent with worship of Jesus, he makes a clear line of demarcation:

"Ye cannot drink the cup of the Lord, and the cup of devils: ye cannot be partakers of the Lord's table, and of the table of devils. Do we provoke the Lord to jealousy? are we stronger than he?" (1Co 10:21-22)

At this point, we see clearly what Paul thinks about the idolaters' *'knowledge'*. It was never true *'knowledge'*, for true knowledge never contradicts the law of love (1Co 8:1-13).

But let us take up his reasoning again. What does Paul say to the argument that there is only one God and no idols, as the Old Testament clearly states (in 1Sa 2:2, for example)? Paul does not question that fact, and even agrees that the externals of the idols, the image and the sacrifices brought to them, are nothing. Idol worship, however, is actually worship of Satan and of his demons:

"But I say, that the things which the Gentiles sacrifice, they sacrifice to devils, and not to God: and I would not that ye should have fellowship with devils." (1Co 10:20)[293]

The Old Testament also clearly teaches that idolatry worships demons (Lev 17:7; Dt 32:17; 2Chr 11:15; Ps 106:37; cf. in the New Testament: 1Co 10:20, Rev 9:20-21, Rev 18:2-3), thus warning against idolatry with all severity, as God requires in the First Commandment (Ex 20:1ff; Dt 5:6-10)[294], but also mocking the images, that can neither speak, hear or aid (Ps 115:4-7; 135:15-17; Isa 44:9-17; Jer 10:3-9; Hab 2:18-19; Ex 32:4; 1Ki 12:28).[295] The Bible also forbids us to mock Satan or his demons (2Pe 2:10-11; Jude 9:10). Whether we cite only the Old Testament teaching that there is only one God who owns all of Creation, or only the teaching that worshipping idols is actually worshipping demons, when we only regard one side, we abandon the truth of Scripture.

The Other Side: Paul on meat sacrificed to idols (1Co 10:24-33)

Now Paul turns to the other party. His statements in 1Co 10:24-33 are no longer directed against those who participated in sacrifices to idols, but against those who tried to avoid contact with sacrificial meat at all costs. Paul in no way intends to carry the warning against worshipping demons over to the meat itself. He had just declared that the images were nothing. If the image itself is only matter, how much less dangerous is the meat which is afterwards sold in the market? Because everything in the world belongs to God (1Co 10:26), Christians may eat anything without having to first investigate its origins. Even when a non-believer

---

[293] Psalm 94:20 mocks the idea of an alliance with the 'throne of disaster'.

[294] This doctrine was also common in Judaism, see Paul Billerbeck, *Die Briefe des Neuen Testamentes und die Offenbarung Johannis erläutert aus Talmud und Midrasch*, Kommentar zum Neuen Testament aus Talmud und Midrasch vol. 3, ed. Hermann L. Strack, Paul Billerbeck (München: C. H. Beck, 1926). pp. 51-52. Judaism also taught that the heathen gods were demons, but that they were also 'nothings' (the Old Testament term), see ibid., pp. 53-60.

[295] See e.g. my books *Marxismus – Opium für das Volk?* (Berneck: Schwengeler Verlag, 1990): pp. 26-29 and *Die Vielfalt biblischer Sprache* (Bonn: VKW, 1997). ct. 'Spott', 'Ironie' etc.

serves meat to a Christian, the guest may eat everything (1Co 10:27).

Paul makes only one exception. If the host points out that the meat is from the pagan temple worship, then the Christian should refuse, in order to make it clear that he refuses to honor or worship other gods (1Co 10:28). But the apostle immediately emphasizes that one should refuse, not because eating the meat would be a sin, but to avoid the confusion it would cause the other: *"But if any man say unto you, This is offered in sacrifice unto idols, eat not for his sake that shewed it, and for conscience sake: for the earth is the Lord's, and the fulness thereof: Conscience, I say, not thine own, but of the other: for why is my liberty judged of another man's conscience?"* (1Co 10:28-29). Paul wishes, above all, that Christians not offend others unnecessarily, especially when the offense is due to something perfectly permissible (1Co 10:29-11:1). Paul argues here just as in Ro 14 and 15, although we must note that his comments in Romans do not concern sacrificial meat, but only similar problems.

Example: The Gifts of the Spirit (1Co 12-14)

Spiritual gifts were another issue which divided the Corinthian church. One group considered all ecstatic behavior permissible, while the others blocked the Holy Spirit's work by objecting to everything enthusiastic or supernatural. Paul opposes both sides and recalls them to the divine order.

Towards those who considered all ecstasy spiritual, Paul points out the danger of confusing the Holy Spirit with pagan practice (1Co12:2-3). God's Spirit can never curse Jesus. Love (1Co 13) and an orderly, understandable worship (1Co 14) are much more important than spiritual gifts.

"And the spirits of the prophets are subject to the prophets. For God is not the author of confusion, but of peace, as in all churches of the saints." (1Co 14:32-33).

At the same time, Paul must continually re-emphasize the importance of spiritual gifts which come from God (12:3-7) and are *profitable* (12:7) for the edification of the church.

The example of the gift of tongues demonstrates that Paul had two errors to refute. One party believed this gift to be the most important of all (12:4-31). To them, Paul replies, *"Do all speak with tongues?"* (12:30). Without love, the gift of tongues is worthless (13:1), and at best, it is of less value than the gift of prophecy (1Co 14).[296] So that speaking in tongues does not dominate the worship service, only two or three members should speak (1Co 14:29), and then only if a translator is present (14:28).

On the other hand, Paul confirms that speaking in tongues is a true gift of the Spirit (12:10,28-31) which he has also received and often uses (14:18). He exhorts the church to *"desire spiritual gifts"* (14:1), and states clearly *"Forbid not to speak with tongues"* (14:39). The gift of prophecy is, however, of greater importance, especially when it can be given without requiring a translator (*"Yet in the church I had rather speak five words with my understanding, ... than ten thousand words in an unknown tongue"*, 1Co 14:19)

4.3. Paul's Corinthian Opponents

To investigate the currents of opposition against Paul in Corinth would go beyond the scope of this work. In seeking concrete movements, theologians have often overlooked the fact that Paul stands between two groups which both argue from the same basic idea. A typically Gnostic division of body and spirit, for example, led to a complete justification of any kind of physical activity on the one hand, but to extreme asceticism on the other. We must, therefore, give up the idea that Paul only had one, clearly defined movement to oppose. Normally, [297] interpreters have assumed

---

[296] Jürgen Kuberski, "Der Text von 1.Korinther 14 in Gegenüberstellung," *Bibel und Gemeinde 89,* no. 3 (1989): pp. 319-326.

[297] See Jerry L. Sumney, "Identifying Paul's Opponents: The Question of Method in 2Corinthians," *Journal for the Study of the New Testament Supplement Series 40* (Sheffield: Almond Press, 1990): pp. 13-68; Dieter Georgi, *Die Gegner des Paulus im 2. Korintherbrief: Studien zur religiösen Propaganda in der Spätantike, Wissenschaftliche Monographien zum Alten und Neuen Testament 11* (Neukirchen, Germany: Neukirchener Verlag, 1964): pp. 7-16.

that Gnosticism lay behind the Corinthian parties.[298] Hans Conzelmann prefers to speak of a "Gnosis in statu nascendi"[299] or
designates Paul's opponents as "Proto-Gnostics",[300] since we
have no documentation for Gnosticism in its pure form until later.
R. Mcl. Wilson has pointed out that the question of Gnostic origins for the Corinthian problems depends on our definition of
Gnosticism. The early usage of the terms 'knowledge' (Greek
'gnosis') and 'wisdom' (Greek 'sophia') may represent the be-
ginnings of a Gnostic movement which later blossomed into a
full-fledged philosophy.[301] Mark Wyndam writes,

"This proto-Gnosticism is exemplified nowhere better than in
the Apostle Paul's 'First Letter to the Church at Corinth'."[302]

---

[298] Richard A. Horsley, "Conscientiousness and Freedom among the Corinthians:
1Corinthians 8-10," *The Catholic Biblical Quarterly 40* (1978): pp. 574-589; Hans von
Campenhausen. "Die Askese im Urchristentum," p. 114-156 in: Hans von Campenhausen, *Tradition und Leben: Kräfte der Kirchengeschichte* (Tübingen: J. C. B. Mohr,
1960): p. 139; W. Schrage, *Die konkreten Einzelgebote der paulinischen Paränese*
(Gütersloh, Germany: Gütersloher Verlagshaus G. Mohn, 1961): p. 113ff; H.- D.
Wendland, *Die Briefe an die Korinther. Das Neue Testament Deutsch 7.* (Göttingen,
Germany: Vandenhoeck & Ruprecht, 1972[13]), p. 54; Chr. Maurer, "Ehe und Unzucht
nach 1Kor 6,12-7,7," *Wort und Dienst 6* (1959): p. 160ff; O. Merk, *Handeln aus Glauben: Die Motivierungen der paulinischen Ethik, Marburger Theologische Studien 5*
(1968): pp. 102-103; Wilhelm Lütgert, *Amt und Geist im Kampf: Studien zur Geschichte des Urchristentums, Beiträge zur Förderung christlicher Theologie 15* (1911)
4/5 (Gütersloh, Germany: C. Bertelsmann, 1911): p. 48-49 u. a. (see Ibid, pp. 92-106
on Gnosticist influence on New Testament Corinth).

[299] I.e. 'Gnosis in the state of its birth'. For the history of Gnosticisms see: Carl Immanuel
Nitzsch, "Die Gesamterscheinung des Antinomismus oder die Geschichte der philoso-
phierenden Sünde im Grundriß," p. 315-404 in: Carl Immanuel Nitzsch, *Gesammelte Abhandlungen*, vol. 2 (Gotha, Germany: F. A. Perthes, 1871), pp. 369-404.

[300] Hans Conzelmann, *Der erste Brief an die Korinther*, op. cit., p. 30.

[301] R. Mcl. Wilson. "How Gnostic were the Corinthians?," *New Testament Studies 19*
(1972): pp. 65-74; W. Edward Glenny, "1Corinthians 7:29-31 and the Teaching of
Continence in *the Acts of Paul and Thecla*", *Grace Theological Journal* 11 (1991): pp.
53-70, here p. 56-57 who appeals to R. Mcl. Wilson and F. F. Bruce, rejects the view
that the Corinthian problems had to do with pre-Gnostic philosophy, and suggests that
the issue was a general adaptation to pagan society. Glenny, however, fails to note that
Wilson emphasizes the significance of the terms, 'knowledge', 'wisdom' etc. in the
Corinthian vocabulary.

[302] Mark Wyndham, "Gnostic Dualism and the Origins of the Medieval Definition of
Witchraft," *Journal of Christian Reconstruction 1* (1974) 2 (Winter): pp. 87-111, here
p. 103. He uses 1Co 6,12; 10,23; 8,1-3; 10,6-8; 11,20-22 und 1Co 5:1,17 as examples.

Hellenistic-Judaistic philosophy (such as Philo or the *Wisdom of Solomon*) may also have influenced the Corinthians.[303] Dieter Georgi has concluded that Paul's opponents in 2Corinthians may have been Jewish enthusiasts in the tradition of Jewish missionaries.[304]

The debate between these opponents can be found in all parts of both epistles. J. C. Hurd has identified Corinthian slogans in 1Co 1:12; 2:14; 6:12; 8:1,4,8; 10:23; 11:2; 14:34-35; 15:12 etc. [305]

Let's take a look at three of these slogans in 2Co, since we are concerned with 1Co.

Dieter Georgi uses 2Co 3:4-18 as an example of Paul's technique of refuting his opponents by repeating their arguments and either using them either polemically or taking them to extremes.[306]

Francis T. Fallon has demonstrated that the catch-phrase 'sufficient' (2Co 2:16) came from the Corinthians.[307] Paul does not con-

---

[303] Richard A. Horsley, "Conscientiousness and Freedom among the Corinthians," op. cit., p. 575 (note 3 further proponents); Richard A. Hosley, "Wisdom of Words and Wisdom of Wisdom in Corinth," *The Catholic Biblical Quarterly 39* (1977): pp. 224-239; see also: Richard A. Horsley, "Pneumatikos vs. Psychikos: Distinctions of Spiritual Status among the Corinthians," *Harvard Theological Review 70* (1977): pp. 269-288; Richard A. Horsley. "'How can some of you say there is no resurrection of the dead?': Spiritual Elitism in Corinth," *Novum Testamentum 20* (1978): pp. 203-231; Richard A. Horsley, "Gnosis in Corinth: 1Corinthians 8,1-6," *New Testament Studies 27* (1980): pp. 32-51.

[304] Dieter Georgi, *Die Gegner des Paulus im 2. Korintherbrief*, op. cit., esp. pp. 114-115+125-126+205-206. Georgi believes the opponents in 2Co to be a different party than those in 1Co He also assumes that 2Co consists of various fragments which detracts from the unity of his argument.

[305] J. C. Hurd, *The Origin of I Corinthians,* op. cit., pp. 61-74 + 154-169; a similar list in Neal M. Flanagan, Edwina Hunter Snyder, "Did Paul put down women in 1Cor 14: 34-36?" *Biblical Theological Bulletin* (New York) 11 (1981): pp. 10-12, here p. 11. Hurd's study is still the most thorough investigation of the citations and allusions in 1Co and on the parties in Corinth.

[306] Dieter Georgi, *Die Gegner des Paulus im 2. Korintherbrief*, op. cit., pp. 258-282. See particularly his discussion of the Greek Text on p. 282, where he attempts to reconstruct the opponents' text which is the basis of 2Co 3, 7-18 , and points out Paul's polemics and irony.

[307] Francis T. Fallon, "Self's Sufficiency or God's Sufficiency: 2 Corinthians 2:16," *Harvard Theological Review 76* (1983): pp. 369-374 refers to Dieter Georgi, *Die Gegner des Paulus im 2. Korintherbrief*, op. cit., p. 221-223.

sider himself as 'sufficient' as his oh-so-sufficient' opponents! The most familiar piece of irony must be 2Co 12:13:

"For what is it wherein ye were inferior to other churches, except it be that I myself was not burdensome to you? forgive me this wrong."

John H. Yoder has shown that Paul also cites his adversaries in order to refute them in 2Co 5:11-17, and that the text can only be understood from this standpoint.[308]

I tend to agree with Gordon D. Fee's suggestion that the Corinthian letter which Paul is answering in 1Co 7:1-16:12 is a reaction to his earlier letter (1Co 5:9). Fee believes that they had not asked for spiritual advice, but were replying to his admonitions on the basis of their own 'knowledge' and 'wisdom'.[309]

Before we deal with concrete instances in 1Co, we must add a few words about Paul's use of humor and irony. Irony, humor, even jokes, are common in both Testaments, but are often rejected as 'unchristian' by critical theologians and by Christians[310] whose serious attitudes contradict the biblical facts[311] which

---

[308] John H. Yoder, "The Apostle's Apology Revisited," pp. 115-134 in: William Klassen, ed., *The New Way of Jesus: Essays presented to Howard Charles* (Newton Kansas: Faith and Life Press, 1980).

[309] Gordon D. Fee, *The First Epistle to the Corinthians. The New International Commentary on the New Testament* (Grand Rapids, MI: Wm. B. Eerdmans, 1987) pp. 266.

[310] The view of Rudolf Bultmann, Karl Barth and Hans von Campenhausen that irony and humor are not compatible with the nature of Christianity, is outdated. For example: Hans Freiherr von Campenhausen. "Ein Witz des Apostels Paulus und die Anfänge des christlichen Humors," pp. 102-108 and "Christentum und Humor," pp. 308-330 in: Hans Freiherr von Campenhausen, *Aus der Frühzeit des Christentums: Studien zur Kirchengeschichte des ersten und zweiten Jahrhunderts* (Tübingen, Germany: J. C. B. Mohr, 1963). Many of the church fathers believed that certain Scriptures were intended to be ironic. Chrsysostomos, for example, believed that that imperative in 1Co 6:4 was ironic, see Lukas Vischer, *Die Auslegungsgeschichte von 1Kor 6,1-11: Rechtsverzicht und Schlichtung,* Beträge zur Geshichte der neutestamentlichen Exegese vol. 1, (Tübingen: J. C. B. Mohr, 1955), p. 34.

[311] See the following studies of biblical humor in : Jakob Jónsson, "Humour and Irony in the New Testament: Illuminated by Parallels in Talmud and Midrash," *Zeitschrift für Religions- und Geistesgeschichte*, add. 28 (Leiden: E. J. Brill, 1985), on the Corinthian epistles: pp. 227-241+260-262; Werner Thiede, *Das verheißene Lachen: Humor in theologischer Perspektive* (Göttingen, Germany: Vandenhoeck & Ruprecht, 1986), on the epistles to the Corinthians: pp. 112-114; G. B. Caird, *The Language and Imagery of the Bible* (London: Duckworth, 1980): pp. 51+104-105+134; See my reviews in "Bi-

demonstrate humor and irony to be significant methods of counseling and instruction.[312] Louis Kretz, in his investigation of Jesus' use of humor, concludes:

"Jesus made jokes not only in passing, not only on minor matters. We observe that he often expressed high thoughts, the very
highest, to express the very core of his doctrine in words drip-
ping with wit. The joke does not detract from the seriousness of
the issue; on the contrary, it elevates the statement and its grav-
ity. Sometimes, it is the humor which clarifies the matter. It is
therefore not at all erroneous to look for humor in Jesus' words.
This method leads not away from the Word, but towards it."[313]

He continues by dealing with a concrete discussion between
Jesus and the Pharisees:

"Jesus knows not only how to turn aside the threats and the
scorn, he also succeeds in beating his enemies, and this with a
minimum of energy, without tension, friendly, but ironic. He
does nothing, but this: He takes literally those of the Pharisees'
words which confirm His own, as if they had been spoken
truthfully ..."[314]

---

belwissenschaft konkret," *Gemeinde Konkret Magazin 5* (1986): p. 1; Louis Kretz,
Witz, Humor und Ironie bei Jesus (Olten, Swiss/Freiburg, Germany: Walter-Verlag:
1982[2]); Edwin M. Good, *Irony in the Old Testament* (Philadelphia, USA, The West-
minster Press: 1950); Yehuda T. Radday, Athalya Brenner, ed., *On Humour and the
Comic in the Hebrew Bible, JSOT Supplement Series* 92 = *Bible and Literature* 23
(Sheffield, U.K., Sheffield Academic Press, 1991[Pb]); Ralph Woodrow, *Noah's Flood,
Joshua's Long Day and Lucifers Fall: What Really Happened?* (Riverside, USA:
Ralph Woodrow Evangelistic Association, 1984) pp. 120-121; Robert H. Stein, *Diffi-
cult Sayings in the Gospels: Jesus' Use of Overstatement and Hyperbole*, (repr. from
1985, Grand Rapids, Michigan: Baker Book House, 1989); compare also my review in
Bibel und Gemeinde 91, no. 4 (1991): p. 446.

[312] Many of the Church Fathers understood certain verses of Scripture to be ironic.
Chrysostomos found the imperatative in 1Co 6:4 ironic, for example. See: Lukas
Vischer, *Die Auslegungsgeschichte von 1Kor 6:1-11*, op. cit., p. 34.

[313] Louis Kretz, *Witz, Humor und Ironie bei Jesus*, op. cit., p. 14-15.

[314] Ibid., p. 113 zu Mt 22,34-40 and Lk 10,25-28, pp. 102-117. On Jesus' use of irony
and hyperbole see: Robert H. Stein, *Difficult Sayings in the Gospels: Jesus' Use of
Overstatement and Hyperbole*, op. cit.

A collection of ironic passages in Paul's writings demonstrates how much Paul had learned from the Old Testament prophets, masters of irony and healthy mockery, and from Jesus, his master.

Irony is a fine, concealed mockery which tries to hit its goal by obtaining exaggerated agreement in order to make it laughable. One idea is thought through all its consequences, and the necessary conclusion drawn, even when, and just because, this consequence is absurd.[315]

I am not interested in detailed definitions of such terminology, such as irony, mockery, humor, sarcasm or polemics, although all these can be found in the Bible. I am concerned with the components of these devices used in counseling. My conclusions do not depend on the details of definition.

Several examples from the Old and the New Testament will suffice to demonstrate these rhetoric devices. The following quotations are not meant to be taken literally; they mean the opposite of what they say, in order to uncover truth in contrast to their absurdity.

Examples of irony and humor in the Old and New Testaments
Job 12:2 to his friends, *"No doubt but ye are the people, and wisdom shall die with you."*
Eze 28:3: The LORD to the princes of Tyre (Satan?) *"Behold, thou art wiser than Daniel; there is no secret that they can hide from thee."*
La 4:21: *"Rejoice and be glad, O daughter of Edom ..., that dwellest in the land of Uz; the cup* (of judgement) *also shall pass through unto thee: thou shalt be drunken, and shalt make thyself naked ..."* (The details of the judgement are described before and after this verse.)
Mk 7:9: *"And he said unto them, Full well ye reject the commandment of God, that ye may keep your own tradition."* (Jesus does not find it 'well' at all!)

---

[315] Irony must be distinguished from sarcasm and mockery.

2Co 11:7-8: *"Have I committed an offence in abasing myself that ye might be exalted, because I have preached to you the gospel of God freely? I robbed other churches, taking wages of them, to do you service."*

2Co 12:13: *"For what is it wherein ye were inferior to other churches, except it be that I myself was not burdensome to you? **Forgive me this wrong.**"*

1Ki 18:27-28: *"And it came to pass at noon that Elijah mocked them, and said, Cry aloud: for he is a god; either he is talking, or he is pursuing, or he is in a journey, or peradventure he sleepeth, and must be awaked. And they cried aloud, and cut themselves after their manner with knives and lancets, till the blood gushed out upon them."*

Zec 11:13: *"And the LORD said unto me, Cast it unto the potter: a goodly price that I was prised at of them. And I took the thirty pieces of silver, and cast them to the potter in the house of the LORD."*

Jdg 10:14: *"Go and cry unto the gods which ye have chosen; let them deliver you in the time of your tribulation."*

Ac 23:3-5: *"Then said Paul unto him, God shall smite thee, thou whited wall: For sittest thou to judge me after the law, and commandest me to be smitten contrary to the law? And they that stood by said, Revilest thou God's high priest? Then said Paul, I wist not, brethren, that he was the high priest: for it is written, Thou shalt not speak evil of the ruler of thy people."* (i.e.: "How should I know that he is the High Priest? He is disobeying the Law!"[316])

Other examples **Isa 17:3; Am 4:4.5; 1Co 4:8**

---

[316] Paul of course knew that he was speaking to the High Priest, for he said, "You sit there, to judge me." Besides, he could recognize the High Priest by his official dress and his seat. In the apostle's eyes, the High Priest had forfeited his office by not keeping the Law.

4.4 Quotations and Irony in 1Corinthians

1Corinthians 7

Most interpreters have long understood 1Co 7:1 to represent
Paul's opinion which he introduces with "*It is* good for a man not
to touch a woman."[317]

Three facts contradict this conclusion:

1. In all cases in which Paul introduces a section with the words
   'about' ('Peri de'), he states his subject expressly[318] (1Co
   7:25: *"about virgins"* 8:1: *"about meat sacrificed to idols"*
   12:1; *"about spiritual gifts"*; 16:1: *"about the collection for
   the saints"*; 16:12: *"About Apollos"*). This characterizes other
   New Testament texts as well.[319]

2. The expression, "to touch a woman", frequently translated
   with *'to marry'*, is a typical Greek euphemism[320] for sexual
   intercourse, as Gordon D. Fee has demonstrated.[321] Paul is
   thus not dealing with marrying but with sexual intercourse.

3. Paul is not dealing with sexual intercourse, but with its profit-
   ability in marriage. His sharp equalization of man and woman
   in sexual matters in 7:2-6 seem to refute the arguments of
   those ascetic Corinthians who denied all earthly things, including sexuality in marriage. In verse 7, Paul states expressly that
   he would prefer for all to remain single as he is, but that both
   marrying and not marrying are *gifts* of God. In the whole chapter, he places great value on marriage and sexuality.[322] If mar-

---

[317] Even E. Kähler, *Die Frau in den paulinischen Briefen*, Dissertation (Zürich, Swiss: Gotthelf-Verlag, 1960): pp. 16-17 assumes that V. 1 states Paul's opinion and not that of the Corinthians. See also: Ibid., pp. 17-21 for her good representation of the text of 1Co 7.

[318] See also David E. Garland, "The Christian's Posture Toward Marriage and Celibacy: 1Corinthians 7," *Review and Expositor 80* (Louisville, USA: 1983): pp. 351-362, here, pp. 351+360.

[319] *'Peri de'* in 1Th 4:9; 5:1; compare: *'peri gar'* in 2Co 9:1.

[320] A 'prettier' word for an offensive expression.

[321] Gordon D. Fee, "1Co 7: 1 in the NIV," *Journal of the Evangelical Theological Society 23* (1980): pp. 307-314, here pp. 307-308; Gordon D. Fee, *The First Epistle to the Corinthians*, op. cit. 274-276.

[322] See: X. Léon-Dufour, "Marriage et virginité selon saint Paul," *Christus 42* (Paris: 1964): pp. 179-194.

riage is a gift of God, how can it be 'good' for a person to 'not touch a woman'?

Besides the possibility that Paul's statement is positively meant, William E. Phipps suggests alternative interpretations:[323]
1. In 1Co 7:1b, Paul is quoting a Corinthian opinion which he then refutes.[324]
2. In 1Co 7:1b, Paul is quoting a Corinthian opinion which he then confirms. [325]
3. 1Co 7:1b is a question which either includes a citation of the letter from the church, or formulates the church's question.[326] Phipps is certain that the verse does not represent Paul's opinion, for the apostle contradicts the idea very clearly.[327]

As far as I know there has been only one attempt to harmonize verse 1, as a statement, with the following verses. Norbert Baumert considers verse 1 Paul's answer, but believes that 'to not touch a woman' means 'to separate oneself – once – from his wife.'[328] Paul, however, questions this very idea in the following verses.

Baumert's conclusion well expresses the problem we do not only have with 1Co 7, but with the whole book, including chapter 11:

"If we only had the church's list of questions, we would be better able to understand the letter! Now we must draw conclusions from Paul's epistle about the questions he is answering. What did the Corinthians ask?"[329]

---

[323] William E. Phipps, "Is Paul's Attitude Toward Sexual Relations Contained in 1.Cor 7.1?" *New Testament Studies 28* (1981) 82: pp. 125-131, here pp. 127-129.

[324] Ibid. p. 128, cites David Smith, *The Life and Letters of Paul* (New York: Harper & Row, 1920): p. 262; as the first proponent. See his list on p. 131, note 22.

[325] On p. 127 he mentions Origen (3rd c.) as the first proponent. Compare p. 127, note 16.

[326] Ibid., cites William Orr, James Walther, *1Corinthians* (New York: Doubleday, 1976): p. 205, as the first proponent.

[327] Ibid., pp. 128-129.

[328] Norbert Baumert, *Ehelosigkeit und Ehe im Herrn: Eine Neuinterpretation von 1Kor 7. Forschung zur Bibel* (Würzburg, Germany: Echter Verlag, 1984): p. 21; See also Norbert Baumert, *Frau und Mann bei Paulus*, op. cit., p. 29-62.

[329] Ibid., p. 29.

Recent interpreters increasingly reject the idea that 7:1b is Paul's answer without first trying to sketch the question or at least the Corinthian question behind it. According to David E. Garland, "there is, however, increasing agreement that Paul must be quoting a catchword of the Corinthian party"[330].

If we understand the statement as a question or as a quotation,[331] the text is saying either, *"As far as the matter in your letter is concerned, 'It is good for a man to not touch a woman'"* or *"Is it good for a man to not touch a woman?"* The question was not intended to deal with sexuality in general, but with marriage, so that the 'woman' means 'the wife'. Perhaps engaged couples[332] were also concerned.[333]

---

[330] David E. Garland, *The Christian's Posture Toward Marriage and Celibacy*, op. cit., p. 351.

[331] See: Gordon D. Fee, "1Corinthians 7: 1 in the NIV," op. cit.; Gordon D. Fee, *The First Epistle to the Corinthians*, op. cit., p. 272-279; W. Edward Glenny, "1Corinthians 7:29-31 and the Teaching of Continence in *the Acts of Paul and Thecla,*" *Grace Theological Journal 11* (1991): pp. 53-70, here p. 59; John C. Hurd, *The Origin of 1Corinthians*, op. cit., pp. 63-64+161-163 (A table on p. 68 lists further recent and older proponents.); David E. Garland, *The Christian's Posture Toward Marriage and Celibacy,* op. cit., p. 351; Neal M. Flanagan, Edwina Hunter Snyder. "Did Paul put down women in 1Cor 14: 34-36?" op. cit., pp. 10-11; F. F. Bruce, *1 and 2Corinthians,* op. cit., p. 66 refers to Origen; D. R. Cartlidge, "1Corinthians 7 as a Foundation for a Christian Sex Ethic," *Journal of Religion 55* (1975): p. 220; On 1Cor. 7, see also: Robin Scroggs, "Paul and Eschatological Woman". *Journal of the American Association for Religions* (JAAR) 40 (1972): pp. 283-303, here p. 294-297; C. K. Barrett, *A Commentary on The First Epistle to the Corinthians,* (London: A & A Black, 1971²), pp. 153-155.

[332] J. K. Elliott, "Paul's Teaching on Marriage in 1Corinthians: Some Problems Considered," *New Testament Studies 19* (1972/73): pp. 219-225; Norbert Baumert, *Ehe und Ehelosigkeit im Herrn,* op. cit., follows Maria Siglinde Zimmermann, "'Jeder, wie Gott ihn ruft': Ein neues Verständnis des Apostels Paulus," *Geist und Leben 58* (Würzburg: Echter, 1985): pp. 455-459. Both attempt to prove that the expression 'virigin' in 1Co 7 should be translated 'fiancee'; the following verses do not question marriage, but rather the dissolution of an engagement to marry.

[333] I assume that the issue in 1Co 7 was sparked off by the expectation that Christ would return soon (1Co 7:26-32) which implied not the end of the world, but the not so distant persecution and the decline of Judaism in the Jewish Wars and the destruction of Jerusalem. 1Co 7:26 speaks of the 'present distress', 7:28 of 'trouble' which plays a role in the 'Great Tribulation' of Mt 24:21 and Mk 13:19. 1Co 7:29 states that the time is short, so that the text does not concern the distant future. The statement in verse 31, 'the fashion of this world passes away' does not, in my opinion, refer to the end of the world, but to the end of the Jewish age. On the expectations of an immediate return of Christ in 1Co 7 from a critical viewpoint, see: Jeremy Moiser, "A Reassessment of Paul's View of the Marriage

The question remains whether verse 2 belongs to the Corinthian question or not. I believe so; in verse 2, the Corinthians are explaining that they are married in spite of their rejection of sexuality (in contrast to other members who proclaimed sexual liberty on the basis of a separation of body and soul – see the following section on 1Co 6) just in case they were to become 'fleshly'. This would make a good transition to the reply in 7:3ff.[334]

Gordon Fee assumes that Paul is repeating a statement in the church's letter.[335] After the one party had expressed its opinion in 6:12 *("everything is 'lawful'")*, now the other party claims the opposite in 7:1.[336] For this reason, we need to investigate 1Co 6:12-13.

Note that 1Co 7 clearly gives men and women equal rights in sexual matters.[337] *"Let the husband render unto the wife due benevolence: and **likewise** also the wife unto the husband. The wife hath not power of her own body, but the husband: and **likewise** also the husband hath not power of his own body, but the wife"* **(1Co 7:3-4)**. Equality is not founded in an egotistical right to self-determination, but in the mutual submission of both partners to each other, the man to his wife, and the wife to her husband.

1Corinthians 6:12-13[338]

The best known slogan in the Corinthian church must have been *"Everything is lawful!"* (6:12; 10:23). Commentators who see Pauline theology in this idea land in difficulties, for Paul ob-

---

with reference to 1Cor. 7," *Journal for the Study of the New Testament* (Sheffield) 18 (1983): pp. 103-122, and a summary of the essay in *New Testament Abstracts* 28 (1984): p. 38.   For a general discussion of the issue from a non-ciritical point of view, see: William R. Kimball, *What the Bible says about the Great Tribulation: Future or Fulfilled?* (Grand Rapids, Michigan: Baker Book House, 1983); David Chilton, *Paradise Restored. An Eschatology of Dominion* (Tyler: Dominion Press, 1985); David Chilton, *The Great Tribulation* (Forth Worth: Dominion Press, 1987).

[334] On 1Cor 7:3ff, see X. Léon-Dufour, "Marriage et virginité selon saint Paul," op. cit.

[335] Gordon D. Fee. The First Epistle to the Corinthians. op. cit., 30-31.

[336] Ibid., p. 30.

[337] Norbert Baumert, *Frau und Mann bei Paulus*, op. cit., p. 39.

[338] Already the previous verses could have an ironic significance. So understood Chrysostomos 1Co 6:4 as an ironic imperative (see Lukas Vischer, *Die Auslegungsgeschichte von 1Kor 6,1-11*, op. cit., p. 34).

viously refutes the statement, taking it to absurd extremes with bitterest irony.[339]

Hermann Menge places the Corinthian slogans in quotation marks and begins Paul's replies with *"Yes, but ..."* His excellent translation of our text well expresses Paul's bitter irony:

"Everything is allowed"
Yes, but not everything is beneficial.
"Everything is allowed"
Yes, but I must allow nothing to control me.
"Food is for the stomach, and the stomach is for food."
Yes, but God will put an end to both.
The body is not for immorality, though, but for the Lord, and the Lord is for the body.

Jerome Murphy-O'Connor has shown how Paul refutes the Corinthians arguments by placing 1Co 6:13 (left) across from 6:14 (right):

"(13)	(14)
- food for the stomach	*- the body ... for the Lord*
- the stomach for food	*- and the Lord for the body*
- but God will	*- but God has*
- them both	*- the Lord*
- destroy	*- raised."[340]*

1Corinthians 8-10

This section must be treated as a unit.[341] The failure to realize that Paul cites his opponents in order to refute them leads to difficulties with phrases such as, *"Everything is lawful"* and with the contrast between *'love'* and *'knowledge'* in 8:1 ("Knowledge puf-

---

[339] See Jerome Myrphy-O'Conner, "Corinthian Slogans in 1Cor 6:12-20," *Catholic Biblical Quarterly 40* (1978): pp. 391-396.

[340] This is a slightly modified imitation from Ibid., p. 394, (there it is in Greek).

[341] For a good presentation of the continuity in 1Co 8-10 see: Gordon Fee, "*Eidolotuta* once Again: An Interpretation of 1Corinthians 8-10," *Biblica 61* (Rom, 1980): pp. 172-197; Richard A. Horsley, "Conscientiousness and Freedom among the Corinthians," op. cit.; Richard A. Horsley, "Gnosis in Corinth: 1Co 8,1-6", op. cit.; H. S. Songer, "Problems Arising from the Worship of Idols: Corinthians 8:1-11:1," *Review and Expositor 80* (1983): pp. 363-375.

feth up, but charity edifieth."), for Paul considers neither wisdom nor knowledge negative, but prays that the churches will receive these gifts. In 2Corinthians, he refutes his opponents with his own knowledge! If 'Knowledge' (Gr. *'gnosis'*) is a Corinthian slogan, and if their 'knowledge' included permission to visit prostitutes, since that only affects the body, and if such 'knowledgeable' people felt justified in participating in idolatrous practices, *then Paul refutes this false knowledge with love and with true knowledge, for "If any man think that he knoweth any thing, he knoweth nothing yet as he ought to know."* (8:2).

Hermann Menge's German translation makes the discussion between Paul and the Corinthians more vivid: (*Paul's comments are in print, his citations of the Corinthian position in italics*)

(1) *"As far as the sacrificial meat is concerned, we know that we all have (sufficient) knowledge."*[342]

Yes, but knowledge makes you arrogant, whereas love edifies. (2): whoever thinks that he knows anything, *still knows nothing as he ought to know.;* (3) *whoever loves God, is known by Him.*

(4)"As far as eating sacrificial meat is concerned, we know that there is no such thing as a false god, and that there is no (other) God but the One.[343] *(5) For although there be so-called gods, whether in heaven or in earth – just as there are (really) many such gods many lords,) – (6) But for us (Christians) there is only one God, the Father, of whom are all things, and we in him (or for him) ; and one Lord Jesus Christ, by whom (or through His mediation) are all things (or have become), and we by him."*[344]

---

[342] For reasons to understand 1Co 8,1 as a quotation of the Corinthians compare: Jerome Murphy-O'Conner, "Freedom of the Ghetto (1 Cor., VIII,1-13; X,23-XI,1)," *Revue Biblique 85* (1978): pp. 543-574, here p. 545+547.

[343] For justifications to understand 1Co 8,4 as a quotation of the Corinthians compare Ibid.

[344] For justifications to understand 1Co 8,6 as a quotation of the Corinthians compare: Jerome Murphy-O'Conner, "I Cor., VIII,6: Cosmology or Soteriology?" *Revue Biblique 85* (1978): pp. 253-267, esp. pp. 254-255.

(7)Yes, but not all (Christians) have such knowledge, for some, because of their (previous) habits, still eat the meat as a sacrifice dedicated to an idol, thus defiling their consciences which are weak enough as it is.

> (8) *But meat does not affect our relationship to God: if we do not eat, we are no worse off, and if we eat we are no better off.*[345]

(9) *Yes, but watch out that by any means this liberty of yours does not become a stumblingblock (or 'offense') to the weak. (10) For if anyone see you, with your* 'knowledge' *eating meat in the idol's temple, won't his conscience be "edified" (or moved) to eat meat in the idol's temple, as well? 11) Your knowledge will thus cause the weak one to perish, the brother for whom Christ died! (12) If you sin against your brother in this way and you maltreat his conscience like this, you sin against Christ. (13) Therefore, if food (what I eat) offends my brother (causes him to sin),* I prefer to do without meat for all eternity, *in order to avoid offending my brother.*" (1Co 8:1-13. English translation from the German translation by Hermann Menge)

Paul continues to use this method of citing the Corinthians and developing their ideas to extremes in chapter 10 as well. Richard A. Horsely, writing about 10.25-27, says,

> "… moreover, as so often in 1 Corinthians, Paul is here playing with words and coaxing the enlightened Corinthians along by using their own languages, only to give it a very different twist or application."[346]

More quotations were mentioned several times before. Not mention were the baptism for the dead in 1Co 15:29. The immense problematic explanation of this passage solves Jerome

---

[345] For justifications to understand 1Co 8,8 as a quotation of the Corinthians compare: Jerome Murphy-O'Conner, "Food and Spiritual Gifts in 1 Cor. 8:8," *Catholic Biblical Quarterly 41* (1979): pp. 292-298 and Jerome Murphy-O'Conner, "Freedom of the Ghetto (1 Cor., VIII,1-13; X,23-XI,1)," op. cit. p. 547.

[346] Richard A. Horsley, "Conscientiousness and Freedom among the Corithians," op. cit., p. 587.

Murphy-O'Conner by understanding 1Co 15,29 as a quotation of the Corinthians. So Paul overtakes but not justifies it.[347]

1 Corinthians 14:34-35

These verses, traditionally understood to forbid women to speak in church meetings,[348] have also been interpreted as repetitions of the Corinthian position, for they contradict the previous statement, *"For ye may all prophesy one by one,"* (1Co 14:31) and the permission given women to prophecy and pray (11:13; cf 11:5). Besides, the following verses could also be refutation of the ban and an admonition to the men: *"What? Came the word of God out from you? Or came it unto you only?"* (14:36). The complete text might look like this:

"For God is not (a God) *of disorder, but* (a God) *of peace, as in all the churches of the saints.*

> *Let the women be still in the churches, for you do not allow them to speak, but they should submit, as the law states. If they want to learn, let them ask their own husbands, for it is shameful for a woman to speak in church.*

But did the word of God originate with you (men or Corinthians) *or did it come to you alone"* (1Co 14:33-36)

[I connect 1Cor 14,33b "nor do the churches of God," to 14:33a. Along with Daniel C. Arichea, and others, I assume that 1Co 14:33b belongs to the previous statement, and not to 14:34a, because Paul would be repeating the expression "As in all the congregations of the saints," and "in the churches" within one sentence. [349] Arichea points out that many translations have rendered the text in this way, including the King James Version

---

[347] Jerome Murphy-O'Conner, "'Baptized for the Dead' (I Cor., XV,29): A Corinthian Slogan?" *Revue Biblique 88* (1981): pp. 532-543, esp. pp. 529+534+535.

[348] A thorough defense of the traditional view can be found in: Archibald Robertson, Alfred Plummer, *A Critical and Exegetical Commentary on the First Epistel of St Paul to the Corinthians,* op. cit., pp. 324-328 and – also against the quotation theory – Arthur Rowe, "Silence and the Christian Women of Corinth: An Examination of 1Corinthians 14:33b-36", *Communio viatorum* (Ecumenical Institute of the Comenius Faculty, Prag) 33 (1990) vol. 1-2, pp. 41-84.

[349] Daniel C. Arichea, "The Silence of Women in the Church", *Bible Translator 46* (1995), pp. 101-112, pp. 102-104.

which certainly cannot be accused of kowtowing to the twentieth century zeitgeist.]
Let me introduce a few proponents of the quotation theory.[350]
Neal M. Flanagan and Edwina Hunter find it significant that Paul

---

[350] **A chronological listing of representatives of the citation interpretation of 1Co 14:34-36, as far as known to me:**

Jessie Penn-Lewis, *The Magna Charta of Woman* (repr. 1975, Bornemouth. U.K.: The Overcomer Book Room, 1919).

Katharine Bushnell, *God's Word to Women* (Oakland: published by the author: n.d., ca. 1918); Ibid., 1930, Paragraphs 189-215.

Katharine Bushnell, *101 Questions Answered: A Womans Catechism – God's Word to Women* (Southport, U.K., Lowes Ltd.: n.d., ca. 1930): p. 23-26.

John A. Anderson, *Women's Warfare and Ministry: What Saith the Scriptures?* (Stonehaven, U.K.: David Waldie, 1933): pp. 20-26.

Katharine Bushnell, *Was sagt Gott der Frau* (Berlin, 1936).

Katharine Bushnell, *The Badge of Guilt and Shame* (Southport, U.K.; n.d.).

Ernestine von Trott zu Solz, *Die Stellung der Frau nach der Bibel* (Asendorf: Land-heim Salem e.V.: n.d.): p. 33-37.

J. C. Hurd, *The Origin of ICorinthians* (New York: Seabury, 1965): p. 186-195.

Joyce Harper, *Women and the Gospel,* C. B. R. F. Occasional Paper 5 (Pinner, U.K.: Christian Brethren Research Fellowship: 1974): pp. 14-19+8-9.

Jessie Penn-Lewis, *The Magna Charta of Woman* (repr. from 1919, Minneapolis: Bethany House Publ.:, 1975): pp. 21-34.

Walter C. Kaiser, Jr., "Paul, Women, and the Church," *Worldwide Challenge 3* (1976) Sept: 9-12.

Neal M. Flanagan, Edwina Hunter Snyder, "Did Paul put down women in 1Cor 14: 34-36?" *Biblical Theological Bulletin 11* (New York, 1981): pp. 10-12.

David W. Odell-Scott, "Let the Women Speak in Church: An Egalitarian Interpretation of ICor. 14.33b-36," *Biblical Theology Bulletin 13* (New York, 1983): pp. 90-93.

C. H. Talbert, "Paul's Understanding of the Holy Spirit: The Evidence of 1Corinthians 12-14," *Prespectives in Religious Studies 11* (1984): pp. 95-108, here pp. 105-107.

Chris Ukachukwu Manus, "The Subordination of the Women in the Church: 1Co 14:33b-36 Reconsidered," *Revue Africaine Théologie 8* (1984) 16 (Oct) pp. 183-195.

David W. Odell-Scott, "In Defense of an Egalitarian Interpretation of 1Cor 14.34-36," *Biblical Theology Bulletin 17* (1987) 3, pp. 100-103.

Robert W. Allison, "Let Women be Silent in the Churches (1Cor. 14. 33b-36): What Did Paul Really Say, and What Did it Mean," *Journal for the Study of the NT 32* (1988): pp. 27-60.

Gilbert Bilezikian, *Beyond Sex Roles: A Guide for the Study of Female Roles in the Bible* (Grand Rapids, Michigan: Baker Book House, 1989[2]): pp. 144-153.

Daniel C. Arichea, "The Silence of Women in the Church," *Bible Translator 46* (1995), pp. 101-112.

uses the masculine form in verse 36. If he had been addressing the women, why did he not use the feminine?[351]

Daniel C. Arichea and Chris Ukachukwu Manus have demonstrated that the particle 'he' in 1Co 14:36 introduces an emphatic contradiction to the previous statement (for example in 1Co 11:22).[352]

Robert W. Allison has also investigated the appeal to the Law in verse 24. He concludes that the Old Testament never requires women to be silent, whereas the conclusion in verse 34 corresponds to the rabbinical exegesis of Ge 3:16 which we have already observed in the Talmud which is then reflected in 11:2-16. Jesus and Paul both contradict the rabbinical interpretation on the basis of the Old Testament.

Joyce Harper and John A. Anderson assume that the appeal to the Law corresponds to the Talmud's ban on women speaking, and that not Paul is appealing to the Law, but that Jewish teachers were appealing to their own erroneous interpretation of the Law.[353] They cite the Talmud with the words,

"It is a shame for a woman to let her voice be heard among men."[354]

S. Aalen came to the same opinion, for he has discovered that the formulation, "it is not allowed" is typical of rabbinical laws and bans.[355]

Jerome Murphy-O'Conner, "Interpolations in 1 Corinthians," *Catholic Biblical Quarterly 48* (1986): pp. 90-92, considers the quotation theory a possibility.

[351] Neal M. Flanagan, Edwina Hunter Snyder, "Did Paul put down women in 1Cor 14: 34-36?" op. cit., pp. 10+12.

[352] Daniel C. Arichea, "The Silence of Women in the Church", op. cit., p. 109 and Chris Ukachukwu Manus, "The Subordination of the Women in the Church: 1Co 14:33b-36 Reconsidered," op. cit., p. 189.

[353] Robert W. Allison, "Let Women be Silent in the Churches (1Cor. 14. 33b-36)," op. cit., pp. 44-45. See also Archibald Robertson, Alfred Plummer, *A Critical and Exegetical Commentary on the First Epistle of St Paul to the Corinthians*, op. cit., p. 325 refers to Gen. 3,16, but assume that Paul had understood (or misunderstood) the text in this way.

[354] Joyce Harper, *Women and the Gospel,* op. cit., p. 14 (from the *Megilla*, a volume of the Talmud), pp. 24-26.

Gilbert Bilezikian lists the following points which suggest that 14:34-35 are quotations from a Corinthian letter:[356] 1) the abrupt change of subject[357]; 2) the contradiction to 11:2-16[358]; 3) the context which teaches that *all* should participate in the worship service (14:31), that *all* should strive for spiritual gifts (14:39)[359]; 4) Paul never appeals to the Law[360] – which however is not valid. This statement fails to correspond to the next argument as well; 5) the Old Testament never commands the woman to be silent.[361]; 6) the Greek 'e' in 1Co 14:36 introduces a strong contradiction,[362] as many texts in the epistle show (6:1-2; 6:9; 6:19; 19:9; 10:22; 11:13; 14:36)[363]; 7) the abrupt change from the feminine in verse 35 to the 2nd person masculine in verse 36[364]; 8) the existence of many similar citations in 1Co (1:12; 3:4; 6:12=10:23; 6:13; 6:18; 8:1; 8:4; 8:8)[365].

H. Talbert summarizes the reasons for the quotation theory[366] as following:

"Two arguments make such a reading probable. First, in vs. 36 the term translated "only" (*monous*) is masculine plural. This requires some such paraphrase as "you fellows only." If 14:34-35 is Paul's injunction, this masculine reference is out of place. If 14:34-35 is the argument of a group of males in the

---

[355] S. Aalen, "A Rabbinic Formula in ICor. 14,34," pp. 513-525 in: F. L. Gross, ed., *Studia Evangelica II., Texte und Untersuchungen zur Geschichte der altchristlichen Literatur* 87 (Ost-Berlin: Akademie-Verlag, 1964).

[356] Gilbert Bilezikian, *Beyond Sex Roles: A Guide for the Study of Female Roles in the Bible* (Grand Rapids, MI: Baker Book House, 1989²): p. 144-153.

[357] Ibid., p. 145.

[358] Ibid.

[359] Ibid., p. 147.

[360] Ibid., p. 149.

[361] Ibid.

[362] Ibid., p. 151.

[363] Ibid., pp. 248-249.

[364] Ibid., pp. 151-152.

[365] Ibid., p. 248.

[366] C. H. Talbert, "Paul's Understanding of the Holy Spirit," op. cit., p. 105 refers to the "Montgomery translation of the New Testament, early in the century," and to David W. Odell-Scott "Let the Women Speak in Church," op. cit. and Neal M. Flanagan, Edwina Hunter Snyder "Did Paul put down women in 1Cor 14:34-36?," op. cit.

Corinthian community, the masculine reference makes good sense. Second, 14:34-35 is so out of step with Paul's position stated in Gal 3:27-28 and 1Co 11:2-16 that any effort to make them fit is contorted, leading often to a theory of interpolation to get rid of the contradiction. Taking 14:34-35 as a Corinthian assertion and 14:36 as Paul's indignant response yields a coherent position ..."[367]

Because of the problems of the text, several others have declared 1Co 14:34-36, or parts of it, to be a later interpolations from non-Pauline sources.[368] In contrast to the situation in 11:2-26, there are indeed historical grounds for assuming interpolation,[369] although I consider this interpretation insufficient. Jerome Murphy-O'Connor rejects the suggestion of interpolations for

---

[367] Ibid., p. 106.

[368] Gottfried Fitzer, "'Das Weib schweige in der Gemeinde': Über den unpaulinischen Charakter der mulier-taceat-Verse in 1. Korinther 14," *Theologische Existenz Heute 110.* (München, Germany: C. Kaiser, 1963). From evangelical writers: Gordon D. Fee, *The First Epistle to the Corinthians*, op. cit., pp. 699-707, (against: D. A. Carson, "'Silent in the Churches': On the Role of Women in 1Corinthians 14:33b-36," pp. 140-153 in: John Piper, Wayne Grudem, ed., *Recovering Biblical Manhood and Womanhood* (Wheaton, Illinois: Crossway Books, 1991): pp. 141-145; also: Jerome Murphy-O'Connor, "Interpolations in 1Corinthians," *Catholic Biblical Quarterly 48* (1986): pp. 81-84, here pp. 90-92; Elizabeth Schüssler Fiorenza, *Zu ihrem Gedächtnis* (München, Grünewald, Mainz, Germany: Chr. Kaiser, 1988): pp. 287-291; G. W. Trompf, "On Attitudes Toward Women in Paul und Paulinist Literature: 1Corinthians 11: 3-16 and Its Context," *The Catholic Biblical Quarterly 42* (1980): pp. 196-215; Karl Hermann Schelke, "'Denn wie das Weib aus dem Mann ist, so auch der Mann aus dem Weib' (1Kor 11,12): Zur Gleichberechtigung der Frau im Neuen Testament," *Diakonia 15* (1984): pp. 85-90, here p. 87; Hans Conzelmann, *Der erste Brief an die Korinther, Kritisch-exegetischer Kommentar über das Neue Testament 5* (1981[12/2]); (the following contradict Conzelmann: C. K. Barrett, *A Commentary on The First Epistle to the Corinthians* (London: A & A Black, 1968): p. 333 and Mary Evans, *Women in the Bible* (Exeter: The Paternoster Press, 1983): pp. 95-96.

[369] All significant witnesses of the Western text set 1Co 14:34-35 after 1Co 14:40, The conservative Evangelical theologian Gordon D. Fee, *The First Epistle to the Corinthians*, op. cit., pp. S. 699-707 sees the only explanation by assuming 34-35 to have been later insertions. Further text critical arguments for the late origin of verses 34-35 can be found in: Philip B. Payne, "Fuldensis, Sigla for Variants in Vaticanus, and 1Cor 14.35-6," *New Testamen Studies 41* (1995); pp. 240-262. See also the discussion in this journal and the opposing view in Curt Niccum, "The Voice of the Manuscripts on the Silence of Women: The External Evidence for 1Cor 14.34-5," *New Testament Studies 43* (1997), pp. 242-255, and in D. W. Bryce, "As in All the Churches of the Saints", *Lutheran Theological Journal 31* (1997), pp. 31-39.

1Co 2:6-16; 6:14; 11:3-16; 15:31-32; 15:44-48, but does believe that 14:34-35 (and 4:6) are later additions.

The interpolation in 1Co 14:34-35 is supported by the argument that some older manuscripts of the New Testament, especially *D* (Codex Bezae) and the Western family, place the ban on speaking (verse 34-35) after verse 40.[370] Gordon D. Fee points out that no other New Testament text – except the longer sections in John 8 and in Mark 16 – is such a section to be found in other places which can only be explained if the text were originally marginal.[371]

Some of the reasons 'against' 1Co 14:34-36 indicate not a non-Pauline interpolation, but a Pauline 'non-Pauline' citation or description of his opponents' position. Murphy-O'Connor places quotation and gloss beside each other before deciding in favor of the gloss.[372]

Also the argument that the text is clearer without verses 34-35 fails if the verses in question are quotations.[373] We intend to follow Paul's flow of thought, including possible citations, but not to eradicate 'un-Pauline' statements in the historical-critical tradition, as Gottfried Fitzer,[374] who considers 14:34-35 non-Pauline interpolations added to the text from 1Ti 2:11-15.

The central issue for the proponents of the interpolation theory is Paul's appeal to the law.[375] Gottfried Fitzer points out that the Old Testament law includes no corresponding regulations, and that Paul never appealed to the Law in this way.[376] He then refers

---

[370] Gottfried Fitzer, "Das Weib schweige in der Gemeinde," op. cit., pp. 6-7; Gordon D. Fee, *The First Epistle to the Corinthians*, op. cit., pp. 699-701.

[371] Ibid., p. 700.

[372] Jerome Murphy-O'Connor, "Interpolations in 1Corinthians," *Catholic Biblical Quarterly 48* (1986): pp. 81-94, here p. 90-92; see also in Jerome Murphy-O'Connor, *1Corinthians, New Testament Message 10* (Wilmington: M. Glazier, 1979): p. 133.

[373] See, for example, Gordon D. Fee, *The First Epistle to the Corinthians,* op. cit., p. 701 and Gottfried Fitzer, "Das Weib schweige in der Gemeinde," op. cit., pp. 10-11.

[374] Ibid., pp. 35-39.

[375] For example, Jerome Murphy-O'Connor, "Interpolations in 1Corinthians," op. cit., p. 91; Gordon D. Fee, *The First Epistle to the Corinthians*, op. cit., p. 707; Gottfried Fitzer, "Das Weib schweige in der Gemeinde," op. cit., pp. 11-12.

[376] Ibid.

to Otto Michels's compilation of Pauline citation forms,[377] which consist of twelve different formula which are used 74 times (not counting 1Co 14:34), each time followed by a direct or indirect quotation of the text. 1Co 14:34, however, has no quotation. Gordon D. Fee has also noted that Paul otherwise never refers to the Law without expressly declaring which law he is citing.[378] That is of course, no conclusive argument; Paul might well have varied his style. This argument does gain significance since there is no corresponding Old Testament regulation.

Fee further objects, because 1Co 4:34-35 contradicts 11:5 which permits the woman to prophecy in public.[379] 1Co 14:26,31 "all" and "every one" may contribute to the worship service.[380] The quotation theory resolves all these problems, in my opinion.

D. A. Carson uses similar arguments to question some of suggested citations. Quotations in the Corinthian epistles are: 1.) always short; 2.) always followed by a qualification and 3.) always unequivocally and sharply refuted.[381] In all of the examples that we have discussed, the quotation cannot be so clearly proven, as the multitude of interpretations shows. In 1Co 8, Paul repeats

---

[377] Otto Michel, *Paulus und seine Bibel. Beiträge zur Förderung christlicher Theologie,* 2. series, vol. 18 (Gütersloh, Germany: C. Bertlesmann, 1929): p. 72 (add. 2).

[378] Gordon D. Fee, *The First Epistle to the Corinthians*, op. cit., p. 707.

[379] Ibid., p. 702.

[380] Ibid., p. 706.

[381] D. A. Carson, "'Silent in the Churches': On the Role of Women in 1Corinthians 14:33b-36," p. 140-153 in: John Piper, Wayne Grudem, ed., *Recovering Biblical Manhood and Womanhood* (Wheaton, Illinois: Crossway Books, 1991) p. 148; see also pp. 147-150; D. A. Carson, *Exegetical Fallacies* (Grand Rapids, MI: Baker Book House, 1984): p. 38-40 [in opposition to Walter C. Kaiser, Jr. "Paul, Women, and the Church," *Worldwide Challenge 3* (1976): pp. 9-12], D. A. Carson, *Showing the Spirit: A Theological Exposition of 1Corinthians 12-14* (Grand Rapids: Baker, 1987): pp. 127-128 (including notes 47-49). The following oppose the quotation theory; Antoinette Clark Wire, *The Corinthian Woman Prophets*, op. cit., pp. 229-230 (against Neal M. Flanagan, Edwina Hunter Snyder, "Did Paul put down women in 1Cor 14: 34-36?," op. cit.; Gordon D. Fee, *The First Epistle to the Corinthians*, op. cit. pp. 704-705 (assumes that it is a gloss); Norbert Baumert, *Antifeminismus bei Paulus?,* op. cit., pp. 130-132 against the quotation theory applied to 1Co 14. See also: Robert W. Allison. "Let Women be Silent in the Churches (1Cor. 14. 33b-36): What Did Paul Really Say, and What Did it Mean," *Journal for the Study of the NT 32* (1988): pp. 27-60; here pp. 35-39.

several longer trains of thought from the church's letter, not only individual slogans.

Even if 1Co 14:34-35 is an express commandment and not a repetition of a Corinthian position, 'being silent' can only refer to speaking in tongues and prophesying, but not to speaking in general.[382] When Paul commands the prophets to be silent (14:30), no one declares this to be a general ban on speaking, but simply the end of the prophet's immediate speech.

In 1Co 14:32, Paul insists that the *"spirits of the prophets"* be *"subject to the prophets".* The subjection here does not refer to a husband or a wife, but to subjection under God's rules of order,[383] to *"self control".*[384]

Richard and Catherine Clark Kroeger have pointed out that the epistle includes many indications that pagan religions of the community still had a strong influence on parts of the church. Members still participated in sacrifices in the temples (10:20-21) and ate sacrificial meats (8:1-13). At Communion, some became drunk, as was common in Dionysian celebrations (11:21), at which speaking in tongues was also common.[385] In Bacchus (or Dionysus) worship, madness was a sign of worship, but Paul attacked this irrationality in 14:23.[386] Tumult which Paul also objects to (14:33), was typical of this pagan cult.[387] In 13:1, Paul compares human and angelic speech with gongs and cymbals. Screaming, particularly by women, was an integral part of Bac-

---

[382] So z. B. Robert W. Allison, "Let Women be Silent in the Churches (1Cor. 14. 33b-36): What Did Paul Really Say, and What Did it Mean," *Journal for the Study of the NT 32* (1988): pp: 27-60, here p. 35-39.

[383] See Gordon D. Fee, *The First Epistle to the Corinthians*, op. cit., p. 707.

[384] E. Kähler, *Die Frau in den paulinischen Briefen*, Dissertation (Zürich, Swiss: Gotthelf-Verlag, 1960): p. 61 sees no reference to submission under the husband or other men, but only to the rules of worship.

[385] Kari Torjesen Malcolm, *Christinnen jenseits von Feminismus und Traditionalismus* (Neukirchen, Germany: Aussaat Verlag, 1987): pp. 52-53 und Richard und Catherine Clark Kroeger, "Pandemonium and Silence at Corinth," *The Reformed Journal 28* (1978) 6 (Jun): pp. 6-11, here p. 9.

[386] Ibid., pp. 6-7.

[387] Ibid., pp. 9.

chus worship.[388] Paul's first words about spiritual gifts (12:2) re-
call the way the Gentiles are carried away *"unto these dumb
idols"*[389] Accordingly, Paul commands all prophets, including the
women (14:32,35) to exercise self-control and to submit to rules
of order. *"They are commanded to be under obedience"* or "Let
them control themselves!" (14:35)[390] The Greek word *'to speak'*
(*'lalein'*) can also mean 'to speak nonsense' or 'to talk all at
once'.[391]

Paul's instructions in 1Ti 2:11-15 refer to another matter and
will be discussed below.

These suggestions about the possibility that 14:34-35 are not a
quotation cannot hide the fact that there are a multitude of variations of the traditional view.[392] The major idea is that women are
forbidden in general to speak in the presence of men during
church meetings.[393] Some interpreters assume that *'to be silent'*
actually means *'to listen'* which would only apply as long as
someone else was speaking.[394] Others believe that the instructions
only applied to tumultuous services,[395] while others apply the text

---

[388] Ibid., pp. 7.

[389] Ibid., pp. 9.

[390] Ibid.

[391] Ibid., pp. 10.

[392] See the review in Archibald Thomas Robertson, *Word Pictures in the New Testament,* vol. 4, *The Epistles of Paul* (repr. from 1931, Grand Rapids, MI: Baker Book
House, ca. 1980): p. 324-328; Elisabeth Huser, "Die Frau in Gottes Augen," *Fundamentum* (FETA) 2 (1985) pp. 20-45, here pp. 42-44; Antoinette Clark Wire, *The
Corinthian Woman Prophets* (Minneapolis, Fortress Press, 1990): pp. 229-232; Norbert Baumert, *Antifeminismus bei Paulus?*, op. cit., pp. 129-130 and Gordon D. Fee,
The First Epistle to the Corinthians; op. cit., pp. 702-703.

[393] Z.B. H. Wayne House, "A Biblical View of Women in the Ministry: Part 3," *The
Peaking of Women and the Prohibition of the Law, Bibliotheca Sacra* no. 579, 145
(1988): pp. 301-318.

[394] Kari Torjesen Malcolm, *Christinnen jenseits von Feminismus und Traditionalismus,*
op. cit., pp. 52-53 refers to her experiences in China, where Christian women were at
first unable to listen, but continually commented on everything, because they were not
accustomed to such meetings. Arguments made on the basis of similar experiences are,
however, not very decisive.

[395] A. Pérez Gordo, "¿Es el velo en 1Co 11,2-16 símbolo de libertad o de submisión?"
Burgense (Burgo) 29 (1988): pp. 337-366.

to the disturbances caused by women interrupting,[396] which is certainly possible. John Temple Bristow assumes that Paul is objecting to disruptive private conversations during worship.[397] Grudem believes that the text merely excludes women from the testing of prophecy.[398] One widely spread interpretation – which I find hard to believe – suggests that the text refers to uneducated women and thus has no significance for educated women today.[399]

[396] Bruno Schwengeler, *Verschobene Proportionen* (Heerbrugg, CH: Schwengeler Verlag, 1975): pp. 69-71; S. T. Lowrie, "I Corinthians XI and the Ordination of Women As Ruling Elders," *Princeton Theological Review 19* (1921): pp. 113-130, here p. 118.

[397] John Temple Bristow, *What Paul Really Said About Women*, (San Francisco: Harper and Row, 1988), pp. 62-63; Marilyn B. Smith, Ingrid Kern (Ed.), *Ohne Unterschied? Frauen und Männer im Dienst für Gott*, (Giessen: Brunnen, 2000), p. 86; I agree with him.

[398] Wayne A. Grudem, *The Gift of Prophecy in 1Corinthians*, (Lanham USA: University of America Press, 1982): col. 239-255.

[399] M. Adinolfi, "Il silenzio della donna in 1Cor. 14,33b-36," *Bibliotheca Orientalis 17* (1975): pp. 121-128.

5. Further Texts on Woman's Dress and Prayer and Her Submission to Her Husband

In this section, I would like to examine a few other New Testament texts about women in which interpretation and translation play a decisive role, and which, in my opinion, require closer study. It would be a great help if scholars of the biblical languages could ignore both the masculine and the feminine predjudices of our day and could simply assume that the revelation in Scripture about the role of men and women corresponds to the the Order of Creation. Perhaps they can investigate these relevant texts anew.

The following questions are not intended to present any particular view, but merely to stimulate further discussion.

1Timothy 2:9-10[400] and 1Peter 3:3-4

(To the *women*: 1Pe 3:1), *"Whose adorning let it not be that outward adorning of plaiting the hair, and of wearing of gold, or of putting on of apparel; But let it be the hidden man of the heart, in that which is not corruptible, even the ornament of a meek and quiet spirit which is in the sight of God of great price."* (1Pe 3:3-4)[401]; *"I will therefore that men pray every where, lifting up holy hands, without wrath and doubting. In like manner also, that women adorn themselves in modest apparel, with shamefacedness and sobriety; not with braided hair, or gold, or pearls, or costly array; But (which becometh women professing godliness) with good works."* (1 Ti 2:8-10)

---

[400] See Heinz Warnecke, Thomas Schirrmacher, *War Paulus wirklich auf Malta?* (Neuhausen, Germany: Hänssler, 1992) for my arguments in favor of a Pauline origin for the Pastoral Epistles.

[401] On 1Pe 3:1-7 see: Norbert Baumert, *Antifeminismus bei Paulus?*, op. cit., pp. 301-314. Baumert assumes that the text is not dealing with mixed marriages, although the term 'winning' sometimes indicated evangelisation, as in 1Co 9,19-22. In 1Pe 3:1-7, the term is used as in Mt 18,15 or Gal 5,26-6,4) for 'to bring back from a false way', in other words, how a Christian woman was to bring her Christian husband back to the right way which assumes that the woman in such situations could think and act more spiritually than her husband. *Ibid.*, p. 310, Baumert identifies 'likewise' with submission in verse 1.

Do these texts forbid women to wear jewelry or expensive clothing? Many interpreters think so, but reject the ban as antiquated?[402] Or is jewelry permitted,[403] but subjected to the true spiritual adornment of the woman? The latter interpretation seems probable to me, because the formulation of the sentences resemble a certain type of Semiticism which does not substitute one thing for another, but evaluates one thing more highly than the other, as in John 6:27.

Let's look at a few examples from the Old and New Testaments. In Jn 6:27, Jesus says, *"Labour not for the meat which perisheth, but for that meat which endureth unto everlasting life."* He is not forbidding his followers to earn a living, merely putting *higher priority* on spiritual life. Similarly in Mk 9:37 *("whosoever shall receive one of such children in my name, receiveth me: and whosoever shall receive me, receiveth not me, but him that sent me.")* Jesus is not substituting Himself to be a substitute for God. Ge 32:28 will serve as an Old Testament example: *"And he said, Thy name shall be called no more Jacob, but Israel: for as a prince hast thou power with God and with men, and hast prevailed."* God Himself continues, however, to use the name Jacob, although the patriarch's true name is now Israel.

If we assume that the texts about women's adornment use mutually exclusive terms, we will have to forbid *"putting on of apparel,"* for, unlike 1Ti 2:9, Peter speaks only of clothing, not of *"costly" clothing* ("whose adorning let it not be that outward *adorning* of plaiting the hair, and of wearing of gold, or of putting on of apparel;" 1 Pe 3:3). Is the apostle forbidding women to wear clothing in general, or do we need some sort of special explanation for the text?

---

[402] D. M. Scholler, "Women's Adornment: Some Historical and Hermeneutical Observations on the New Testament Passages," *Daugthers of Sarah 6*, no.1 (Chicago, 1980): pp. 3-6.

[403] Homer A. Kent, *The Pastoral Epistles: Studies in I and IITimothy and Titus* (9. repr. from 1958, Chicago: Moody Press, 1977): pp. S. 111-112; Ralph Woodrow, *Women's Adornment: What does the Bible Really Say* (Riverside: Ralph Woodrow Evangelistic Association, 1976): pp. 17-27.

Elisabeth Huser summarizes the Old Testament background of women's dress and adornment as following:

"The Old Testament mentions the woman's *exterior* and her beauty (Ge 24:16; 29:17; SS 4:1; Est 2:7; Job 42:15; Ps 45:13; 144:12), but praises her fear of God more highly (Pr 31:30).

Beautiful clothing and *adornment* are mentioned in a positive context in Ps 45:13-14; Isa 61:10; Eze 16:11-13; Jer 2:32 (the bride adorns herself for the bridegroom); Est 2; SS 5:5. (In the New Testament, a different sort of decoration has higher priority: 1Pe 3:3-4; 1Ti 2:9-10)."[404]

1 Timothy 2:8-10

The question we must answer about this text is, whether Paul wants

1. the men to pray in a particular way (vs. 8) and
2. the women *'in like manner also'* (vs. 9), dress in a particular way

   or whether Paul wants

1. the men to pray in a particular way and
2. *'in a like manner, also'* the women are to pray, but in a particular sort of clothing.

Both interpretations are grammatically possible.

Does the text prescribe a certain kind of dress for all situations or only for public prayer as Church Father Chrystostomos[405] and F. F. Bruce[406] understand it?[407] In my opinion, Paul is discussing the prayers of both men and women, but addresses the typical but wrong attitude shown by both sexes.

---

[404] Elisabeth Huser, "Die Frau in Gottes Augen," *Fundamentum* (FETA) 2 (1985) pp. 20-45, here p. 34. Huser then describes nakedness or the wearing of sackcloth as a punishment, and makeup is usually mentioned in a negative context.

[405] F. F. Bruce, "Women in the Church: A Biblical Survey," *Christian Brethren Review* (Exeter: Paternoster) no. 33 (Dec 1982): pp. 7-14; see also: Katharine Bushnell, *101 Questions Answered.* op. cit., pp. 61-62.

[406] F. F. Bruce, "Women in the Church," op. cit.

[407] This view was proposed before the rise of feminism and is not a mere reaction against it. See Adoniram J. Gordon, "The Ministry of Women," *Missionary Review of the World 7* (1894): pp. 910-921.

Of course, the proper attitude to prayer can also be applied to life in general, but then, it must apply to the man's anger just as much as to the woman's dress. At any rate, I cannot imagine that Paul is requiring only men to raise their hands – i.e. pray – but not women.

1 Timothy 2:11-15

Paul here[408] commands the woman to be silent, *not to teach and rule over the man. She is to be saved in or by childbearing.*[409]

With the word *"and not"* (Gr. 'oude'), Paul is referring

either to 1) teaching and 2)ruling, the woman is thus 1) not to teach and 2) not to rule,[410]

or to one activity,[411] *teaching and ruling* which could be translated as *'not to teach if she rules by teaching.* '[412]

I hold the second opinion and believe that it corresponds to Paul's intention *that the woman is not to teach, if in doing so, she*

---

[408] On the traditional view, see David J. Moo, "1Timothy 2: 11-15: Meaning and Significance," *Trinity Journal* (Deerfield/Illinois) 1 (1980): pp. 62-83; H. Wayne House, "A Biblical View of Women in the Ministry: Part 3," *The Speaking of Women and the Prohibition of the Law, Bibliotheca Sacra* no. 579: 145 (1988): pp. 301-318; in opposition: Herman Ridderbos, *De Pastorale Brieven. Commentaar op het nieuwe Testament* (Kampen: J. H. Kok, 1967): pp. 79-86; K. O. Sanders, "'... et liv som vinner respekt': Et sentralt pa 1Tim 2: 11-15," *Tijdschrift voor Theologie en Kirk 59* (1988): pp. 97-108; S. Jebb, "A Suggested Interpretation of 1Ti 2: 15," *Expository Times 81* (1970): pp. 221-222.

[409] On the affect of this text see: Jürgen Roloff, *Der erste Brief an Timotheus; Evangelisch-Katholischer Kommentar zum Neuen Testament 15* (Neukirchen: Benziger Verlag & Neukirchener Verlag, 1988), pp. 142-146.

[410] This interpretation is also proposed by theologians who consider its application antiquated. See: R. W. Longstaff, "The Ordination of Women: A Biblical Perspective," *Anglican Theological Review 57* (1975): pp. 316-327; K. A. van der Jagt, "Women are saved through bearing children (1Timothy 2. 11-15)," *Bible Translator 39* (1988): pp. 201-208.

[411] On this usage *'oude'* in Greek Grammar, see Richard und Catherine Clark Kroeger, *I Suffer not a Woman: Rethinking 1Timothy 2,11-15 in the Light of Ancient Evidence* (Grand Rapids, MI, Baker Book House, 1992): pp. 83-84+189-192.

[412] Andreas J. Köstenberger, "A Complex Sentence Structure in 1Timothy 2:12," pp. 81-104 in: et al, (Ed.), *Women in the Church: A Fresh Analysis of 1Timothy 2:9-15,* op. cit., pp. 210 has thoroughly demonstrated that teaching and authority which are closely related to each other, must be seen as both positive or both negative, but considers it possible that both are forbidden.

rules over the man. A general ban on teaching is improbable, for Paul refers very positively to female teachers. In Tit 2:3-4; they are commanded to be *"teachers of good things"* who instruct younger women. In 2Ti 1:5 and 3:14-15 they are commanded to teach their children.

The first interpretation is only tenable when we could prove that Paul is only speaking of *public teaching.*

The question is, what does Paul mean by '**ruling**'?[413] The word used here ('authentein') appears in the New Testament only in this verse.[414] The corresponding substantive originally meant 'murderer',[415] specifically 'suicide' or 'family murderer'.[416] It later took on the meaning 'lord', 'ruler' or 'autocrat' in vulgar Greek.[417] The Turkish word 'Effendi' is a derivative.[418] The change in meaning can be explained by the word's undertone, 'to decide independently', ' to act at one's own discretion', 'to act

---

[413] Kari Torjesen Malcolm, *Christinnen jenseits von Feminismus und Traditionalismus*, op. cit., p. 56-58 refering to unpublished sources, translates *'authentein'* with "to seduce someone to sexual relations" (p. 56). She was unable to offer documentation.

[414] The word is not mentioned even as *'hapax legomenon'* in Kittel's *Theologischem Wörterbuch*, but was used by many great classical writers. See N. J. Hommes, "Let Women be Silent in Church," *Calvin Theological Journal 4* (1969): pp. 5-22, here p. 18 as well as the bibliography, a good compilation of Hommes' article in: *New Testament Abstracts 13* (1969): p. 365.

[415] C. D. Osburn, "Authenteo (1Timothy 2: 12)," *Restoration Quarterly 25* (1982), pp. 1-12.

[416] N. J. Hommes, "Let Women be Silent in Church," op. cit., p. 8.

[417] Ibid. and Walter Lock, *A Critical and Exegetical Commentary on The Pastoral Epistles (I & IITimothy and Titus), International Critical Commentary* (Edinburgh: T. & T. Clark, 1936): p. 32 also mentions the vulgar Greek term *'despotes'* (Tyrann) as a meaning for *'authentein'* im Vulgärgriechischen (= 'Despot'), as well as the English "a self-actor", "to lord it over" etc. Sir Robert Falconer, "1Timothy 2 14,15: Interpretative Notes," *Journal of Biblical Literature 60* (1941): pp. 375-379, here p. 375 uses similar terms, „a master, an autocrat". Joseph H. Thayer, *Greek-English Lexicon of the New Testament* (Grand Rapids, MI: Baker Book House, 1977): p. 84. No. 830 suggests for *'authenteo'*: "one who with his own hand kills either others or himself", "one who does a thing himself, the author", "one who acts on his own authority, autocratic" which corresponds to *'autokrator'*, "an absolute master".

[418] N. J. Hommes, "Let Women be Silent in Church," op. cit., p. 18 and the literature mentioned in note 14.

selfishly and inconsiderately'.[419] N. J. Hommes suspects that this text also reflects Paul's frequent irony.[420]

"I suspect that the apostle who certainly liked to use sharp irony, must have enjoyed using this slang expression 'anthentein andros', 'to be bossy over one's husband'."[421]

Richard and Catherine Clark Kroeger[422] have studied the extra-biblical usage of 'authentein' and have concluded that the term did not take on the meaning 'to rule' or 'to usurp power' until the third or fourth century AD.[423] Earlier texts in Attic Greek use the word to mean 'to murder'. Since the time of Euripides, the term had taken on sexual connotations which implied sexual rights, so that the Church Father Chrystostomos used the corresponding noun *authentia* to designate 'sexual permissiveness'.[424]

This would indicate that 1Ti 2:12 is discussing women who were teaching and practicing a fertility cult, dominating men sexually. If this is so, the text could be translated, *"I do not permit a woman to teach* (falsely) *or to dominate the man sexually."* In 2Ti 3:6-7, Paul also deals with sexually permissive women. In Rev 2:20, John condemns the toleration of *"Jezebel which calleth herself a prophetess, to teach and to seduce my servants to commit fornication, and to eat things sacrificed unto idols"* (Compare Rev 2:14; Nu 25:3; 31:15-16).[425] In the same way, Paul ad-

---

[419] David & Elouise Fraser, "A Biblical View of Women: Demythologizing Sexegesis," *Theology, News and Notes* (Pasadena: Fuller Theological Seminary Alumni, June 1975): pp. 14-18, here p. 15; Mary Evans, *Women in the Bible*, op. cit., p. 103.

[420] See N. J. Hommes, "Let Women be Silent in Church," op. cit., pp. 14-15.

[421] Ibid., p. 19.

[422] Richard und Catherine Clark Kroeger, *I Suffer not a Woman: Rethinking 1Timothy 2,11-15*, op. cit. See also the earlier version: Catherine C. Kroeger, "Ancient Heresies and a Strange Greek Verb," *The Reformed Journal 29* (1979) 3 (Mar): pp. 12-14; Richard und Catherine Clark Kroeger, "May Women Teach?" *The Reformed Journal 30* (1980) 10 (Oct): pp. 14-18. A similar view can be found in Faith Martin, *Call Me Blessed: The Emerging Christian Woman* (Grand Rapids: Wm. B. Eerdmans, 1988): pp. 136-142+150-154.

[423] Catherine C. Kroeger, "Ancient Heresies and a Strange Greek Verb," op. cit., p. 12.

[424] Ibid., pp. 12-14.

[425] Ibid.

monishes women who surrender to their *desires, 'tattle'* and lead
disorderly lives and are seduced by men who enter the houses and
kidnap them which was typical of the priests of Cybele.

The Kroegers relate the context of 1Ti 2:12, particularly to the
reference to Eve, to the conflict with Gnosticism in the Pastoral
Epistles. Some Gnostic groups considered women the transmit-
ters of divine revelation, and declared Eve to be the first mediator
of revelation and salvation.[426] Philo of Byblos who died 45 AD,
held   a   similar   view.[427]   In   Ophitic   Gnosticism   (Gr.
'ophis'=serpent) which was closely related to Cybelan fertility
religions and to worship of Isis and Artemis, both Eve and the
serpent were worshipped, as many Church Fathers relate. In the
same way, the Gnostic rejection of birth fits in Paul's argumentation. In 1Ti 5:14, he instructs women involved in these heresies to
marry and bear children.[428]

Important contradictions of this view have been submitted.[429]
Especially the question of the situation in Ephesus and of the
meaning of *'authentein'* have been heavily debated. [430]

For these reason, the authors suggest an alternative translation
for 1Ti 2:12 which emphasizes not the sexual undertones of 'to
rule' but the common root of the Greek *'authentein'* and the term
'author' which are derived from the word for 'origin': *"I do not*

---

[426] Richard und Catherine Clark Kroeger, "May Women Teach?," op. cit., pp. 14-17.

[427] Richard und Catherine Clark Kroeger, "I Suffer Not a Woman," op. cit., p. 65.

[428] Ibid., pp. 161-177.

[429] Andreas J. Köstenberger et. al., (Ed.) *Women in the Church: A Fresh Analysis of
1Timothy 2:9-11,*. op. cit., Köstenberger defends the classical view, and criticizes most
of the positions in this section. The study is thorough, but appears to be determined by
the authors' own interests.

[430] The most vehement advocate of 'murderer' on the base of extrabiblical sources is L.
E. Wilshire, "the TLG Computer and Further Reference to authenteo in 1Timothy
2.12," *New Testament Studies 34* (1988), pp 120-134. The traditional view is defended
by George W. Knight III, "authenteo in Reference to Women in 1Timothy 2.12," *New
Testament Studies 30* (1984), pp 143-157 and H. Scott Baldwin, "A Difficult Word:
authenteo in 1Timothy 2:12," pp. 65-80 and "Appendix 2: authenteo on Ancient Greek
Literature," pp. 269-306 in: Andreas J. Köstenberger et. Al., (Ed.). *Women in the
Church: A Fresh Analysis of 1Timothy 2:9-15,* (Grand Rapids: Baker Books, 1995);
shortened edition in German in: Andreas J. Köstenberger et. al., (Ed.), *Frauen in der
Kirche: 1.Tim 2,9-15 kritisch untersucht,* (Giessen: Brunnen, 1999).

allow a woman to teach and to present herself as the origin (or *author*) *of the man, but she is to behave in an orderly fashion.*"[431]

N. J. Hommes and the Kroegers understand the term **'to be still'** not as **'to be silent'**, but in terms of their interpretation of 'to rule'. After studying the use of the term in both Testaments, they come to the conclusion that 'to be still' means 'to remain within the limits which have been set'.[432]

Does the expression **'to be still'**, when used in reference to women, mean 'not to speak' which 'sigao' can indeed signify (See Lk 14:3), or does it have the more general meaning 'to be peaceful', 'to behave in an orderly way' which is more common in the New Testament? I believe the latter to be the case, for otherwise all Christians, men and women, would have to be silent, as in 1Th 4:11.[433] *"Brethren, ... study to be quiet, and to do your own business, and to work with your own hands, as we commanded you;"* or in 2Th 3:12: *„We ... exhort by our Lord Jesus Christ that with quietness they work, and eat their own bread."*[434]) N. J. Hommes' suggestion is significant here, that 'stillness' here does not concern speaking, but divine order which should not be opposed.[435] Many advocates of the traditional view, such as Thomas R. Schreiner, nevertheless hold this view[436] – refering to 1Pe 3:4 and other texts.

There are four standard views on the meaning of **'salvation through the bearing of children'** (1Ti 2:15 *"Notwithstanding*

---

[431] Ibid., p. 103. Sir Robert Falconer, "1Timothy 2 14,15: Interpretative Notes," *Journal of Biblical Literature 60* (1941): pp. 375-379, here p. 375 relates 'ruling' to public expression of doubt about the man's teaching.

[432] Ibid., p. 20. See also "I Suffer Not a Woman," op. cit., p. 75-76.

[433] Walter Bauer, Kurt und Barbara Aland, *Wörterbuch zum Neuen Testament,* op. cit., col. 707-708; Homer A. Kent, *The Pastoral Epistles*, op. cit., p. 114 suggests that Paul is referring to Eve's usurpation of Adam's authority in the Fall.

[434] See also Ac 11:18 ("When they heard these things, they held their peace,") and 1Ti 2:2 which commends "a quiet and peaceable life" (See also Katherine Bushnell, *101 Questions Answered*, op. cit., pp. 57-58.

[435] N. J. Hommes, "Let Women be Silent in Church," op. cit.

[436] Andreas J. Köstenberger, "A Complex Sentence Structure in 1Timothy 2:12," op. cit., p 12.

she shall be saved in childbearing, if they continue in faith and charity and holiness with sobriety. ")[437]
1. Physical salvation through childbearing
2. Spiritual salvation through childbearing
3. Spiritual salvation through fulfillment of family duties in the home
4. Spiritual salvation through the birth of Christ.

The first three interpretations are possible linguistically, but lead to major doctrinal problems for those who believe in salvation by faith and not by works. The last suggestion would resolve the basic problem that the text seems to create special conditions, works, for the salvation of the woman. Paul would thus be saying that women are saved by *the birth of the child*, Christ.[438] Note that the word for *'child-bearing'* (Gr. 'teknogynia') is not otherwise used for normal birth, and that Paul may have coined it in order to distinguish between the birth of Jesus and other births. Besides, the word is determined by the article (i.e. *'the'* childbearing) which indicates that it is not referring to birth in general but to a specific event, in which God straightened and blessed the woman's road to salvation, when, in fulfillment of the promise given after the Fall, a woman bore Je-

---

[437] See the representation in Homer A. Kent, *The Pastoral Epistles,* op. cit., pp. 115-120.

[438] Homer A. Kent, *The Pastoral Epistles,* op. cit., pp. 118-119; George W. Knight, *Commentary on the Pastoral Epistles. New International Greek Testament Commentary,* (Grand Rapids: Wm. B. Eerdmans, 1992): pp. 147-148, Walter Lock, *A Critical and Exegetical Commentary on The Pastoral Epistles (I & IITimothy and Titus). International Critical Commentary* (Edinburgh: T. & T. Clark, 1936): pp. 32-33; H. von Soden, Hand-Commentar zum Neuen Testament, vol. 3, (Freiburg: J. C. B. Mohr, 1893): pp. 231-232; G. Wohlenberg, *Die Pastoralbriefe. Kommentar zum Neuen Testament 13,* ed. by Theodor Zahn (Leipzig: A. Deichert, 1906): p. 118. (Ibid., note 12 on proponents of the proposition in the history of the church.); A. D. B. Spencer, "Eve at Ephesus (Should women be ordained as pastors according to the First Letter to Timothy 2: 11-15)," *Journal of the Evangelical Theological Society 17* (1974): pp. 215-222; David & Elouise Fraser, "A Biblical View of Women," op. cit., p. 15; Katharine Bushnell, *101 Questions Answered,* op. cit., pp. 66-67; Jeffery J. Meyers, *Does the Bible Forbid Family Planning?: A Biblical and Theological Evaluation of Mary Pride's Arguments Against Birth Control in Her Book The Way Home. Biblical Horizons Occasional Papers 10* (Tyler: Biblical Horizons, 1990, copies): p. 21 (Ibid, further proponents). Further advocates are listed (against his own opinion) by Thomas R. Schreiner, "An Interpretation of 1Timothy 2:9-15", pp. 105-154 in: Andreas J. Köstenberger et. al. (ed.), *Women in the Church: A Fresh Analysis of 1Timothy 2:9-15,* (Grand Rapids: Baker Books, 1995), p. 148, Notes 194-195.

sus Christ, the Savior of the world. This interpretation suits the context which concerns the Fall of Man. In my opinion, Paul is referring to the birth ('the childbearing' of Jesus), as the Church Fathers, Ignatius[439] and Irenaeus[440] and other church fathers[441] believed.

Submission

The term 'submission' requires more study before we can clarify these texts for our day and age. In Tit 1:10, Paul condemns the disorderly, and in both texts, he commands the mutual submission of man and woman before instructing the woman to submit to her husband.

"Submitting yourselves one to another in the fear of God. Wives, submit yourselves unto your own husbands, as unto the Lord" (Eph 5:21-22).

Especially if we want to hold on to biblical the doctrine of the wife's *'submission'* to her husband (Eph 5:21-22, 24; Col 3:18; Tit 2:5; 1Pe 3:1,5) even for today, we must clarify exactly what Scripture means by 'submission'[442] and clearly distinguish between the wife's submission to her husband and other sorts of submission, such as that of children to their parents.

---

[439] Ignatius, 'An die Epheser' 19, cited in Hermann Ridderbos, *Pastorale Brieven*, op. cit., p. 84.

[440] Irenäus, 'Wider die Häretiker' 5,19; cited in Hermann Ridderbos, *Pastorale Brieven*, op. cit., p. 84; Sir Robert Falconer, "1Timothy 2 14,15: Interpretative Notes," *Journal of Biblical Literature 60* (1941): pp. 375-379, here p. 376 writes that the Latin commentators, but not the Greeks, related these words to the 'great childbirth' of the one Mann, Jesus Christ.

[441] Compare Stanley E. Porter, "What Does it Mean to Be 'Saved by Childbirth' (1Timothy 2.15)?," *Journal for the Study of the New Testament 49* (1993) pp. 87-102, p. 90. Jürgen Roloff, *Der erste Brief an Timotheus*, op. cit., p. 140 calls this proposition an "ancient tradition", but rejects it, because the corresponding Messianic interpretation of Ge 3:15 did not arise until the 2nd c. AD in the works of Justin and Irenaeus. As if we possessed sufficient sources to prove that! Not to mention the fact that the Jews were quite familiar with this parallel. Roloff is, at any rate, convinced that this text is referring to Ge 3, Ibid., p. 141.

[442] See also "Let's Look Again at the Biblical Concept of Submission", pp. 135-140 in: Carol J. Adams, Marie M. Fortune, *Violence Against Women and Children: A Christian Theological Sourcebook*, (New York: The Continuum Publ. Comp., 1995), pp. 136-139.

We must observe *that neither* the Old Testament nor the New
ever command *a general submission of women under men, but
only the submission of the wife to her own husband*, as Ephesians
5:21-22 states.
Let me emphasize that the forms of biblical submission can
vary. The submission of children to their parents is different than
the submission of citizens to the State or of employees to their
employers or the of church members to the elders. There is a significant difference between children's submission to parents and
the wife's submission to her husband, even though both pertain to
family life. The Bible requires almost complete obedience of the
child, but only for the first two decades of his life. We must also
note that the Bible otherwise expressly combines authority with
the right to penalize (for example: parents are authorized to punish their children, the church is authorized to discipline its members, etc.), but never authorizes husbands to punish their wives.
The wife is instructed to submit to her husband, but the husband
is not given any right to enforce her obedience. On the contrary,
he is instructed to remember his great responsibility for her, to
love her deeply and to sacrifice himself for her (Eph 5:25-33).
Nor are men by definition more spiritual than women. In both
Testaments women frequently had more spiritual understanding
than their husbands. Samson's mother, for example (Jdg 13:1-25)
recognises the Angel of the Lord although her husband does not.
Zippora, in contrast to Moses, her husband, realises that God's
anger can be appeased by the circumcision of her son (Ex 2:21-2
6). Abigail even disobeys her husband, Nabal who is *"such a
wicked man that no one can talk to him"*. (1Sa 25:17) and "like
his name – his name is Fool, and folly goes with him." (1Sa
25:25). By providing for David's men against Nabal's will, she
averts punisment (2Sa 25:17-31). Other wives make sure that
God's will is done when their husbands are unable to do so. Eli-
asbeth, wife of the Zacharia the priest and mother of John the
Baptist (Lk 1:5-25,39-45,57-64), insists that her son receive the
name that God had chosen (Lk 1:60).

Let's look at several scriptures which compare man and woman. They depict women as independent personalities with intelligence and wisdom – as the image of God.

Let's start with the Fifth Commandment "Honor *your father* **and** *your mother*, so that you may live long in the land the LORD your God is giving you." Jan P. Lettinga writes:

"We notice that both father and mother are mentioned, as so often in biblical laws which indicates the essential equality of the parents."[443]

As examples, he mentions Ex 21:15,17; Lev 19:3; 20:9, Dt 21:18-19 and 27:15. The Book of Proverbs, above all, continually advises the pupil to attend his mother's teaching (Pr 1:8; 6:20). Both man and woman have authority over their children.

The Bible teaches sexual equality as well as pedagogical equality. *"The husband should fulfil his marital duty to his wife, and likewise the wife to her husband. The wife's body does not belong to her alone but also to her husband. In the same way, the husband's body does not belong to him alone **but also** to his wife"* (1Co 7:3-4).

Equality does not give the individual a selfish right to self-determination. On the contrary, it affirms that both spouses belong to each other, not just the woman to her husband.

Scripture teaches cultural equality as well. Women have artistic gifts, compose music, write poetry (including Scriptures! Miriam, Hanna, Debora and Mary composed songs of praise). They are good economists and teach wisdom. That should not come as a surprise, for the cultural commission "Fill the earth and subdue it," is addressed to "Man and Woman" (Ge 1:28).

Evolutionists talk as if all significant cultural achievements, such as religion and social rules were due to men,[444] but fail to present any historical proof. The only feminine achievement they acknowledge is the discovery of language which suppos-

---

[443] Jan P. Lettinga, "Sprachliche Erwägungen zum Text der Zehn Gebote," *Fundamentum* (1990) 1: 37-53 and (1990) 2: 33-50, 2: 39.

[444] See feminist criticism with examples from school and textbooks in: Heide Göttner-Abendroth, *Das Matriarchat I: Geschichte seiner Erforschung*, (Stuttgart: W. Kohlhammer, 1989²), pp. 14-30.

edly arose from the tender sounds mothers made to their children. The biblical view of the world, however, will survive, even if scientists someday prove that a woman started the first fire or made the first wheel!

The Bible also teaches equality between the sexes in their relationship to God. Women are *"heirs with you of the gracious gift of life"*, (1Pe 3:7). Paul reminds us, *"There is neither Jew nor Greek, slave nor free, male nor* female, for you are all one in Christ Jesus"*, (Gal 3:28). He speaks of "spiritual *sisters"* (Ro 16:1; 1Co 7:15; Phm 2; Jas 2:15) and "female fellow workers in Christ" (Ro 16:3; Php 4:3) who worked very hard in the Lord and contended at his side in the cause of the gospel (Php 4:2).

The Bible describes many women who were more spiritual than their husbands (for example, Elkana und Hanna, 1Sa 1; Samson's parents in Jdg 13) who could present biblical truth better than their husbands (for example, the *"prophetess"* and *"judge"* Deborah who had to call Barak to lead the army, Jdg 4:4; and possibly Priscilla in Ac 18:2,18,26; Ro 16:3; 1Co 16:19; 2Ti 4:19; especially Ac 18:26).

God can use women for important commissions.[445] Miriam, Moses' sister was a *"prophetess"* (Ex 15:20), and Micah, speaking of Israel, says: *"I sent Moses to lead you, also Aaron and Miriam"*, (Mic 6:4). Besides, Hannah of the Old Testament, we find the New Testament Hannah who greets the infant Jesus in the Temple (Lk 2:36-38). The prophetess Hulda induces Josiah's reformation (2Ch 34:22). Women served in the Tabernacle (Ex 38:8) and could dedicate themselves to God in a Nazirite vow (Nu 6:2).

The New Testament also has its prophetesses, such Philipp's daughters (Ac 21:9). The prophecy of Pentecost with its accompanying miracles explicitly mentions *'daughters'* and *'maids'* (Ac 2:16-22; Joel 3:1-2). Several women accompanied Jesus, some of whom are mentioned by name (Lk 3 8:1-3). Churches meet in women's houses (Mary, Ac 12:12; Nympha Col 4:15; Lydia Ac

---

[445] Cf. Faith Martin, *Call Me Blessed: The Emerging Christian Woman*, (Grand Rapids: Wm. B. Eerdmans, 1988), pp. 114-125.

16:1-15,40).[446] We have already discussed the deaconate (Ro 16:1; 1Ti 3:11).

It seems important to me that the Bible gives men a particularly authoritative role, but does not base this on any natural superiority. The only natural advantage of men is their physical strength which he is to control (1Pe 3:7).

Men are neither smarter, better, more moral, nobler, responsible, more valuable, more sober or more intelligent than women. Even if they were, these factors are not the basis of his authority. Women are not to submit because of any lack of intelligence, goodness or value. As a matter of fact, God created Woman, because Adam couldn't manage on his own and needed assistance. Now, the distinctive roles of men and women are to be derived from God's commandment and His creative order. Scripture never bases them on any sort of natural precedence, but only in the divine plan for family and marriage which is the only system in which humanity can find true happiness and peace.

---

[446] These may have involved only hospitality.

The Author

Professor Thomas Schirrmacher holds chairs in ethics, in world religions and in international development in Germany, Romania, USA and India, is rector of Martin Bucer Theological Seminary with 11 campuses in Europe and president of Gebende Hände gGmbH (Giving Hands), an internationally active relief organisation. He has authored and edited 74 books, which have been translated into 14 languages.

As an international human rights activist he is on the board of the International Society for Human Rights, manager of the Religious Liberty Commission of the German and the Swiss Evangelical Alliance, and director of the International Institute for Religious Freedom of the World Evangelical Alliance.

He holds the following degrees: M.Th. (STH, Basel, Switzerland), Dr.theol. (Ecumenical Theology & Missiology, TU Kampen, Netherlands), Ph.D. (Cultural Anthropology, PWU, Los Angeles), Th.D. (Ethics, WTS, Lakeland, Florida), Dr. phil. (Sociology of Religion, State University, Bonn, Germany), honorary doctorates: D.D. (Cranmer Theological House, Shreveport), D.D. (ACTS UNIversity, Bangalore, India).

He is listed in Marquis' Who's Who in the World, Dictionary of International Biography, International Who is Who of Professionals, EU-Who is Who, Who is Who in der Bundesrepublik Deutschland, 2000 Outstanding People of the 21st Century, 2000 Outstanding Intellectuals of the 21st Century, International Who's Who in Distance Learning, Kürschners Deutscher Sachbuch-Kalender.

Thomas is married to Christine, a professor of Islamic Studies, and father of a boy and a girl.

Form & Freedom

WHAT THE NEW TESTAMENT TEACHES ABOUT
CHURCH GOVERNMENT AND CHURCH LEADERSHIP

by
JEFF BROWN

In a day when churches are forsaking biblical distinctives, this book provides a clear call back to the New Testament church polity and practice. The material in this book will provide encouragement to those who desire a biblical model for their local church, and pause for those who are looking for guidance beyond the Text to current culture. In Short, Jeff Brown's book is a must read.

Daniel K. Davey, Th.D., Pastor
Colonial Baptist Church, Virginia Beach, Virginia

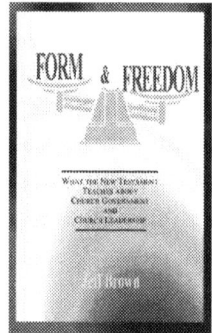

"Jeff Brown has written a very fine volume by building a solid case for his work, not by simply comparing various systems and traditions, but by going directly to the inspired text. I heartily commend it to all who are interested in learning more about God's intention for the governing process of the church."

Earl D. Radmacher, M.A., Th.M, Th.D
President and Distinguished Professor of Systematic Theology Emeritus
Western Conservative Baptist Seminary Portland, Oregon

Paperback · 153 pp. · $12,99 / £10,95 / €12,80
ISBN 978-3-937965-10-9

Order from:
VTR Publications
vtr@compuserve.com
http://www.vtr-online.de

www.ingramcontent.com/pod-product-compliance
Lightning Source LLC
Chambersburg PA
CBHW072155090426
42740CB00012B/2276